FRETBOARD ROADMAPS LAP STEEL GUITAR

THE ESSENTIAL PATTERNS ALL GREAT STEEL PLAYERS KNOW AND USE

BY FRED SOKOLOW

Edited by Ronny Schiff

THE AUDIO TRACKS
Lap Steel, Guitar and Vocals—Fred Sokolow
Recorded, mixed and mastered at
Sossity Sound by Michael Monagan, and
Dennis O'Hanlon Recording and Music Services

PLAYBACK+
Speed · Pitch · Balance · Loop

To access audio visit:
www.halleonard.com/mylibrary
Enter Code
4665-3846-7562-3970

ISBN 978-1-4803-9656-2

HAL•LEONARD®
CORPORATION

7777 W. BLUEMOUND RD. P.O. BOX 13819 MILWAUKEE, WI 53213

In Australia Contact:
Hal Leonard Australia Pty. Ltd.
4 Lentara Court
Cheltenham, Victoria, 3192 Australia
Email: ausadmin@halleonard.com.au

Visit Hal Leonard Online at
www.halleonard.com

CONTENTS

INTRODUCTION

Hawaiian music, country & western, Western swing, rock 'n' roll, blues, sacred steel, swing... The lap steel is heard in all of these genres and has played a significant role in the development of most of them. Going by many names (steel guitar, Hawaiian guitar, lap guitar, etc.), the lap steel is the electric cousin of the Dobro (acoustic lap-style slide guitar) and the predecessor of the pedal steel—and it's the first electric guitar!

Accomplished steel guitarists can play all of the aforementioned styles; they can ad-lib solos and play backup in any key—all over the fretboard—using several open tunings. There are moveable patterns on the fretboard that make it easy to do these things. The pros are aware of these "fretboard roadmaps," even if they don't read music. If you want to play electric lap steel with other people, this is essential knowledge!

You need the fretboard roadmaps if...

- You want a basic understanding of how to navigate in different tunings.

- Some keys are harder to play in than others.

- You can't automatically play any steel lick that you can think of or hum.

- You know a lot of steel guitar "bits and pieces" but don't have a system that ties them all together.

Read on, and many mysteries will be explained. Since you're serious about playing steel guitar, the pages that follow can shed light on it and save you a great deal of time.

Good luck,

Fred Sokolow

THE ONLINE AUDIO

All of the licks, riffs, and tunes in this book are played on the accompanying audio.

There are also four "practice tracks" on the recording. Each track illustrates a specific soloing style, such as "first-position steel licks in open G tuning" or "moveable steel licks in C6 tuning," and all the tracks are mixed with the lap steel on one side of your stereo and the backup band on the other side so that you can tune out the lead guitar and practice playing solos with the backup band.

PRELIMINARIES

Before electric lap steels were available, early Hawaiian, country, vaudeville, and swing guitarists played metal lap-style National steel guitars, wooden Weissenborn models, square-neck Dobros, and flat-top acoustic guitars with raised string action (see below). The tunes and techniques in this book can be played on all of those models, as well as on electric lap steel.

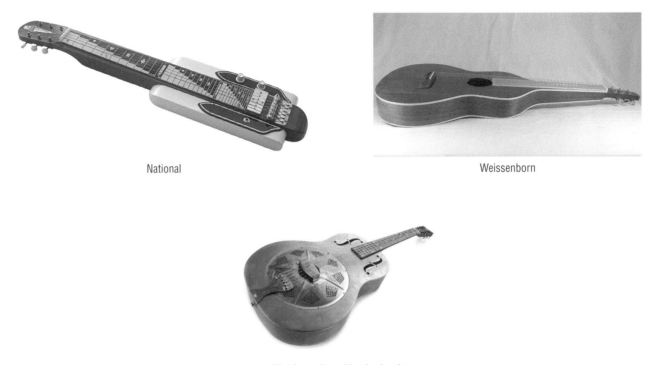

National   Weissenborn

Wooden guitar with raised action

The first widely-used electric steel guitar, perhaps the first ever manufactured, was the early-'30s Rickenbacker "frying pan," so named because it resembled a frying pan with a guitar neck attached.

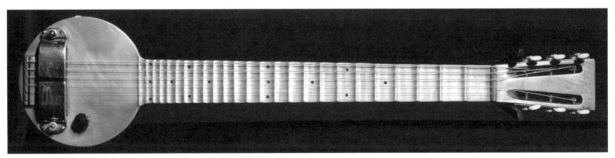

"Frying Pan" Rickenbacker

As manufacturers began offering other models, and players developed more sophisticated styles, seven-, eight-, and 10-string lap steels were created. Doublenecks were created to accommodate different tunings, and the steel guitar was placed on legs, thereby becoming a "table steel." In the late '40s, some manufacturers began adding pedals and knee levers and, by the late '50s, the modern pedal-steel guitar had all but supplanted lap steel in country music, rendering it a "retro" instrument.

In the '70s, lap steels were occasionally seen in rock bands, and eventually new models became available from several instrument manufacturers. Today, lap steels are seen in Western swing, retro swing, country, rock, blues, and, of course, Hawaiian bands. The most popular electric lap steels offered today are six-string models, and that's what we'll deal with in this book. They all need to be amplified, and countless amps are available in different sizes, with different features.

FRET MARKINGS

In lap-style guitar, all notes are fretted with a metal bar—a "steel"—instead of with the fingers. There are no frets, but there are fret markings, which are usually painted on the fretboard. These markings often differ from one another, depending on which fret they indicate, and on some steels, they repeat every 12 frets, as shown below:

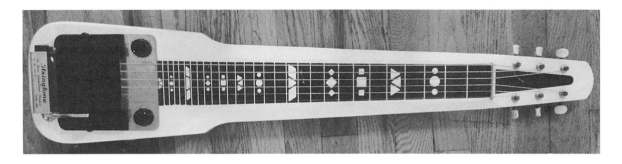

USING A STEEL

Lap-steel players use a variety of steels, including those pictured below. The shape on the left is the most popular.

Steel for lap steel player   "Stevens steel," preferred by Dobro players

- Hold the steel with your thumb, index, and middle fingers, as shown below.

- Rest your pinky and ring finger on the strings, *behind the steel*, to eliminate unwanted noises.

- Fret the strings *lightly* with the steel; don't try to press the strings down to the fretboard.

- Hold the steel *directly* over the fret markings, not between them. Otherwise, your notes will sound flat or sharp.

How to hold the steel

SEVERAL WAYS TO SLIDE

- You can slide up to a note from a few frets below.

- You can slide down from a note.

- You can slide back-and-forth between notes.

- You can play notes without sliding, using your left-hand ring and pinky fingers to dampen the strings.

- You can emphasize or sustain a note by shaking your left hand from the wrist while fretting a string. This gives you a singing vibrato.

All of these techniques are illustrated in the following exercise, which is played in G tuning (see **ROADMAP #1**):

TRACK 1

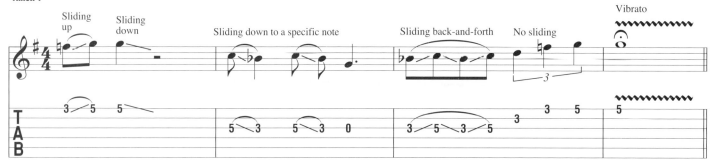

FINGERPICKS

Most lap-steel players use a thumbpick (usually plastic) and two fingerpicks (usually metal). They fit on your picking hand as shown in the picture below:

Fingerpicks

STRINGS

Heavy-gauge strings are preferred, such as sets that have a .014 gauge first string.

TUNINGS

Most players tune the lap steel to an open chord. There are countless lap-steel tunings, and many players invent their own variations. The most common early tuning was open A, and various others evolved over the years, including open D, C6, and E7. When instrument makers started building lap steels with eight or more strings, other tunings, like E9 and E13, came into use, especially among country players. Most lap steels made today have six strings, so this book deals with the most popular and useful six-string tunings.

Here's the good news: many tunings share similar intervals. For example, the interval pattern of the top four strings of one tuning may be duplicated in the middle four strings of another tuning. Therefore, a new tuning does not usually mean starting over from the beginning!

READ THE CHAPTERS IN ORDER, STARTING WITH G TUNING

If you're new to lap slide guitar, it's best to read this book in sequence, because each section builds on the previous section. You'll begin with G tuning because it's probably the easiest starting point and it can be used in any genre. D tuning follows, as it's related to G tuning: with a simple mental adjustment, you can use most of your G tuning skills in D tuning. These tunings, G and D, are used most often by rock and blues players, and G tuning is the most common Dobro tuning, especially in bluegrass.

Next comes E7, one of the most popular "traditional" lap-steel tunings. It's very useful for country and blues and is similar to D tuning (like the G-to-D conversion, a few simple adjustments makes this tuning easy for D-tuning players). Finally, we deal with C6, perhaps the most popular traditional lap-steel tuning. It's very evocative of early country and Hawaiian music. Again, it bears more than a little resemblance to open G, so, if you've developed G tuning skills, C6 is easier to grasp.

G TUNING: FIRST POSITION

Blues Scale

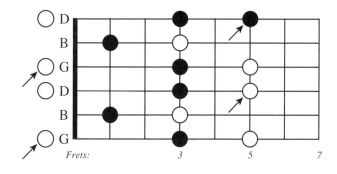

Major Scale

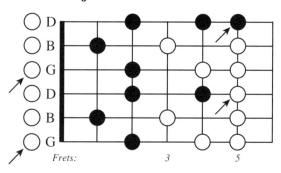

● scale notes
○ alternate notes (see top of next page)

WHY? Very similar to the G tuning used by Mississippi Delta blues players, G tuning is useful in all kinds of music. Once you're familiar with the above scales, you can play countless melodies and licks in first position, in "open G" tuning.

WHAT? **Both of the above diagrams are for G tuning.** When you strum the open (unfretted) strings in this tuning, you play a G major chord. That's why it's often called "open G tuning."

The major scale is the eight-note "do-re-mi" scale on which so much music is based. The blues scale is pentatonic (it consists of five notes). The ♭3rd and 7th are sometimes called "blue notes."

The scales are guidelines. Sometimes other notes (between the notes indicated above) work.

The arrows point out the tonic (G) notes, also called *root* notes. Notice the high tonic note at the fifth fret. Many licks resolve on this note, or on other G notes.

The white dots (circles that are not filled in) are "alternates." They are duplicated by open strings or by higher strings. For example, the fourth string/fifth fret and the open third string are both G. The sixth string/fifth fret and the fifth string/first fret are both C.

HOW? **Here's the tuning, from the sixth to the first string: G–B–D–G–B–D.** Notice that the second, third, and fourth strings duplicate standard guitar tuning. The sixth and fifth strings are tuned higher than in standard tuning and the first string is tuned down:

TRACK 2

Tune the sixth string to G.

Tune the fifth string to B.

Tune the fourth string to D.

Tune the third string to G.

Tune the second string to B.

Tune the first string to D.

Play the scales ascending and descending, starting from a G note.

G Tuning

Blues Scale

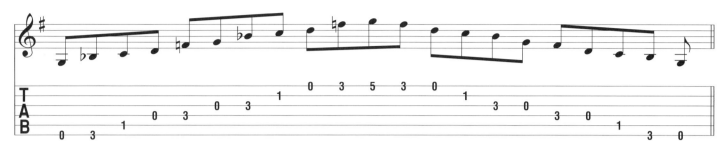

G Tuning

Major Scale

Use the "alternate notes" for sliding or vibrato. You can't slide to an open third string/G note, but you can slide up to the same G note at the fourth string/fifth fret. You can't play vibrato on the open first string/D note, but you can play vibrato on the same D note at the second string/third fret.

DO IT! **Use the blues scale to ad-lib solos throughout a bluesy tune.** In spite of the chord changes in "Rocky Blues," all of the soloing is based on the G blues scale.

ROCKY BLUES

TRACK 3

G Tuning

Use the blues scale to play melodies and blues licks. In the following solo, the guitar plays the melody to the old blues "See, See Rider," including ad-lib blues licks that fill the areas between melodic phrases.

SEE, SEE RIDER

Use the major scale to play melodies and ad-lib solos. In "Chilly Winds," the melody and fills are based on the major scale.

CHILLY WINDS

G Tuning

SUMMING UP—NOW YOU KNOW...

1. How to tune to open G

2. How to play a first-position G major scale

3. How to play a first-position G blues scale

4. How to use both scales to play melodies and ad-lib solos and licks

G TUNING: SOLOING UP THE NECK

G Blues Scale

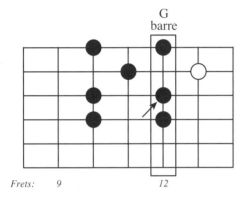

G Major Scale

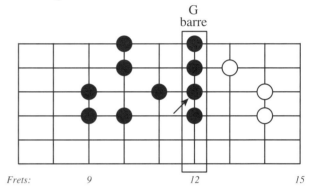

● scale notes
○ alternate notes

G Major Scale

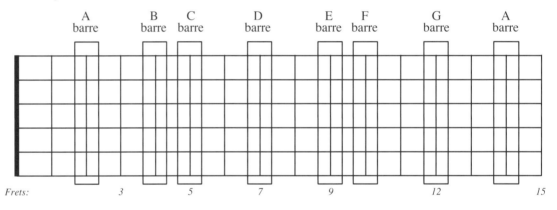

WHY? The scales and chords in **ROADMAP #2** make it possible to solo and ad-lib licks in any key.

WHAT? **The top diagrams show two moveable scales: G major and G blues.** Both scales have the same "home base"—the barred G chord at the 12th fret. (*Barring* means fretting two or more strings at once, at the same fret, by laying a finger flat across the fretboard.) The arrows point out the tonic (G) notes.

The scales are "moveable" because they use no open strings. If you play the G major scale two frets lower (using the barred F chord at the 10th fret for a home base), it's an F major scale.

The white dots are "alternates." They are duplicated by lower notes. For example, the fourth string/14th fret and the third string/ninth fret are both E.

The lower diagram shows the barred major chords in G tuning. You can base licks and solos on these chords, using the moveable scales.

The "sharp" and "flat" major chords are found between the indicated chords. A barre at the sixth fret, one fret above C, is C♯ (D♭). A barre at the eighth fret, one fret below E, is E♭ (D♯).

The fretboard "starts over" at the 12th fret. The G barre at the 12th fret matches the open-string G chord; the 14th-fret A chord matches the second-fret A, and so on.

HOW?

Play the scales ascending and descending, starting from a G note:

G Tuning

Blues Scale

Major Scale

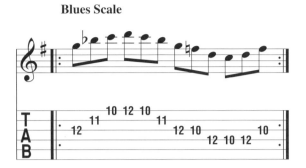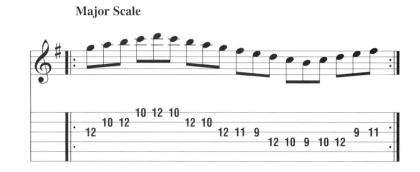

Play both moveable scales in other keys. For example, a barre at the 10th fret is an F chord. Play an F blues scale and F major scale:

F Blues Scale

F Major Scale

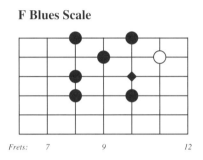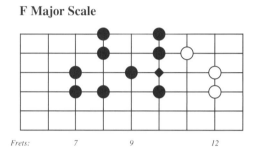

Frets: 7   9   12

Frets: 7   9   12

Harmonize the major scale by playing pairs of notes. Play the fifth and third strings simultaneously, as well as the fourth and second, third and second, and second and first strings:

C Major Scale

G Major Scale

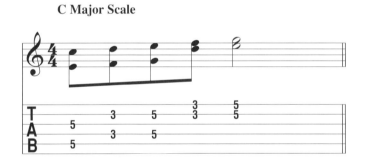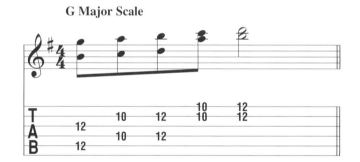

You can play chord-based licks and melodies by following a song's chord changes and playing the appropriate barred chords.

Besides playing the notes of a barred chord, you can play major scale and blues scale notes for each barre.

The first string, five frets above a barre, is a high tonic (root) note. (The first string/10th fret, five frets above the C barre, is a high C note.) This "key note" is often useful in solos.

Before playing a song, make sure that you know where the I, IV, and V chords are located. They are the three main chords in countless songs.

- The I chord is the tonic (G, in the key of G).

- The IV chord is so named because its root is the fouth note of the major scale of the given key. C is the fourth note of the G major scale, so C (or C6, C7, etc.) is the IV chord in the key of G. The IV chord is always five frets above the I chord.

- The V chord is so named because its root is the fifth note of the major scale of the given key. It is always two frets above the IV chord (seven frets above the tonic).

Key of E:

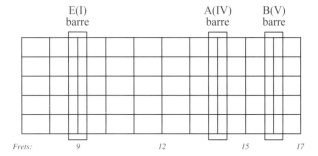

Key of C:

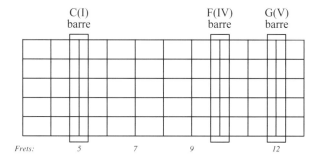

Key of A:

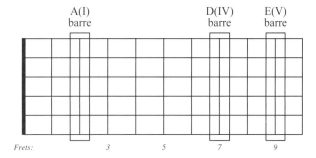

Key of F:

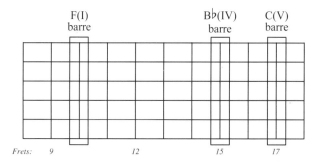

Find other chords (II, ♭VII, VI) by relating them to the I, IV, and V. For example, the II chord is always two frets above the I chord. The ♭VII chord is always two frets below the I chord. The VI chord is two frets above the V.

DO IT!

Use the moveable blues scale to ad-lib solos to bluesy tunes like "Rocky Blues," from **ROADMAP #1.** The entire solo is based on 12th-fret G licks.

ROCKY BLUES II
(at 12th fret)

TRACK 6

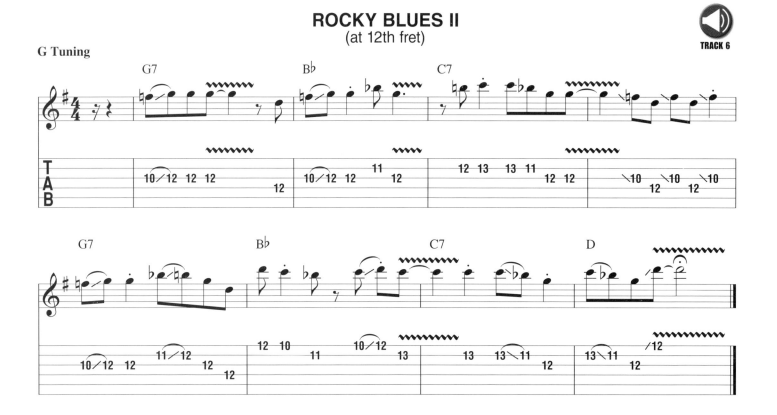

Use the moveable blues scale to play bluesy melodies and licks in keys other than G. "See, See Rider II," which follows, is in the key of E and the entire solo is based on E licks around the ninth fret:

SEE, SEE RIDER II
(Key of E)

G Tuning

Use the moveable major scale to play melodies and solos. Here's a melodic solo to "Amazing Grace" in the key of F (10th fret). Many of the melody notes are harmonized.

AMAZING GRACE

TRACK 8

G Tuning

Use the moveable major scale to ad-lib backup licks to "Red River Valley" in the key of C (fifth fret):

RED RIVER VALLEY

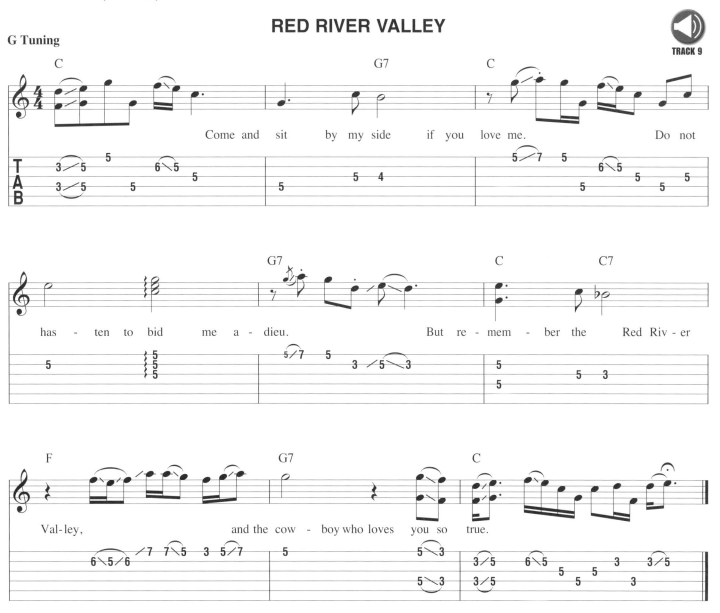

Come and sit by my side if you love me. Do not has - ten to bid me a - dieu. But re - mem - ber the Red Riv - er Val - ley, and the cow - boy who loves you so true.

Play backup and the melody to "Stagolee" in the key of E by following the song's chord changes. Instead of playing at or near the ninth fret throughout, play scale-based licks for each barred chord: E (I) at the ninth fret, A (IV) at the second fret, and B (V) at the fourth fret.

STAGOLEE

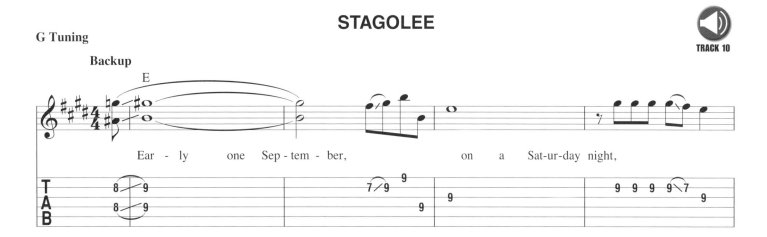

Ear - ly one Sep - tem - ber, on a Sat - ur - day night,

Stag-o - lee   and   Bil - ly De-Ly-ons   had a   ter - ri -ble fight.   He's a

bad - man,   that   cru-el   Stag o-lee.

Solo

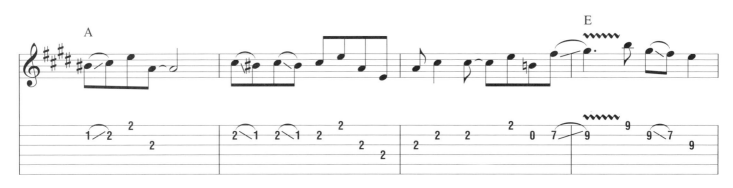

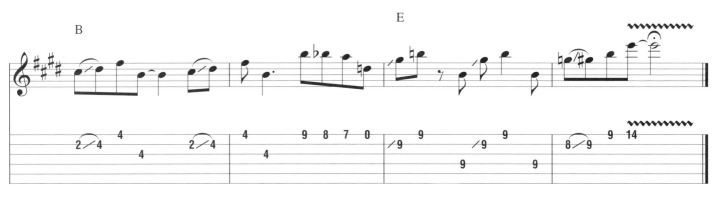

Play a chord-based solo and backup to "Sloop John B." in the key of F. Your barred chords are F (I) at the 10th fret, C (V) at the fifth fret, and B♭ (IV) at the 15th fret. Note the use of "double notes" (as in "Amazing Grace"):

SLOOP JOHN B.

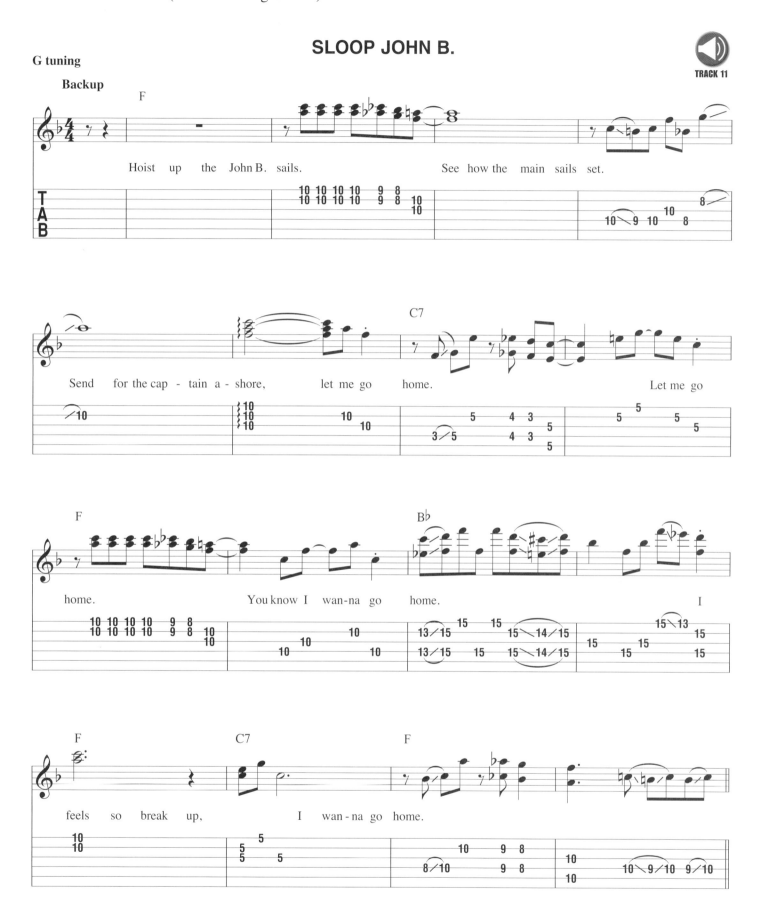

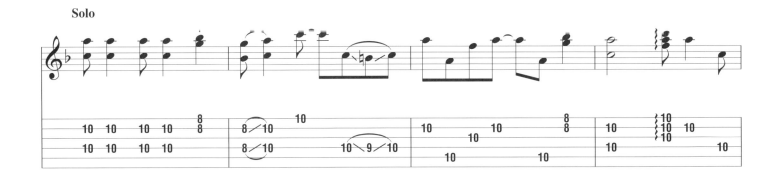

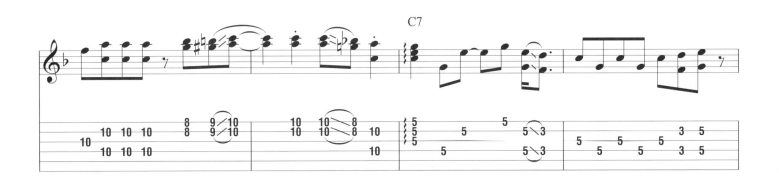

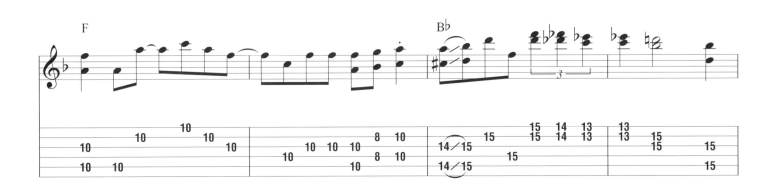

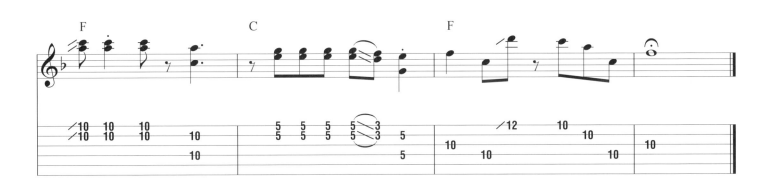

Here's a chord-based solo to the old folk tune "I Never Will Marry," in the key of D. The chords are D (I) at the seventh fret, G (IV) at the 12th fret, and A (V) at the second fret.

I NEVER WILL MARRY

G tuning

This version of "Rocky Blues" is chord-based and includes some harmonized licks. The chords are G (I), B♭ (♭III), C (IV), and D (V).

ROCKY BLUES III
(Chord-Based)

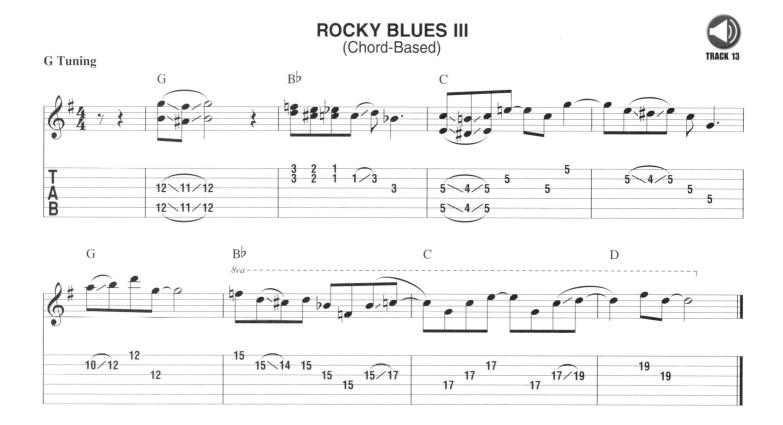

G Tuning

SUMMING UP—NOW YOU KNOW...

1. How to play a moveable major scale in G tuning
2. How to play a moveable blues scale in G tuning
3. How to use both scales to play melodies, solos, and licks in any key
4. How to harmonize licks and melodies by playing note pairs
5. How to play all of the barred major chords in G tuning
6. How to play chord-based solos and backup in G tuning, in any key

G TUNING: SLANTS, MINORS, AND OTHER CHORDS

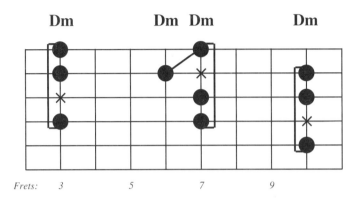

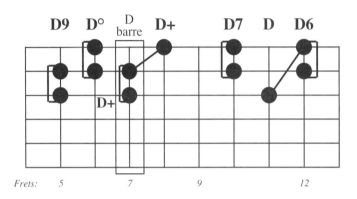

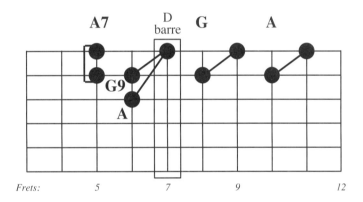

WHY? Many tunes include minor chords, diminished chords, and other chord types. There are some tricks involved in playing them when your guitar is tuned to a major chord. It takes three roadmap diagrams to illustrate all of the chord shapes.

WHAT? **A "slant" chord is played by slanting the steel, instead of holding it perpendicular to the strings.** This enables you to fret one string higher or lower than another string.

All three diagrams show how to find various chord types by relating them to the barred major chord (in these charts, D major). For example, in the second diagram, there's a D7 on the first and second strings, three frets above the barred D chord.

The relationships on all of these charts are moveable. For example, you can turn any major chord into a seventh chord by playing the first and second strings, three frets above the barre.

The first diagram shows several D minor chords (they are actually two- and three-note chord "partials").

The second diagram of ROADMAP #3 shows how to play many D chords (D6, D7, D9, etc.). Each new chord shape can be understood in terms of how it relates to the barred D major chord.

The third diagram of ROADMAP #3 shows how to find certain IV and V chords (G9, A7, etc.) by relating them to the barred D major chord.

HOW?

(Regarding the First Diagram of **ROADMAP #3**, Minor Chords)

By simply not playing the second or fifth strings, you can make any barred chord harmonize with a minor chord. The resulting chord has no 3rd, so it's neither major nor minor, but it doesn't clash with a minor chord:

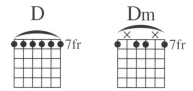

You can turn any barred major chord into a minor chord by slanting back on the second string while playing the first string at the barre. It takes some practice to get the intonation right on slant chords (see photo), but it's worth the trouble.

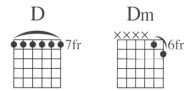

You can make a barred chord minor by playing the first and second strings (or second and fourth or all three strings) four frets below the barre:

 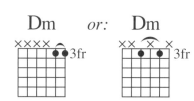

Since the first and fourth strings are tuned to the same note, they are interchangeable in many of these partial chords. Ditto for the second and fifth strings.

There's another way to locate this minor chord: it's one fret above its V chord. In other words, to find a Dm, play the first and second strings one fret above the A barre, because A is a 5th above D. To play an Em, play the first and second strings one fret above the B barre, as B is a 5th above E.

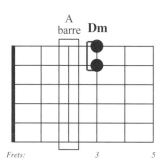

You can make a barred chord minor by playing the second and third (or third and fifth) strings three frets above the barre:

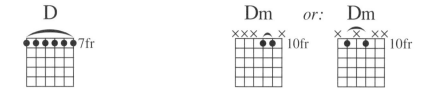

A major chord is so frequently followed by its relative minor (the minor chord that is a 6th higher) that it is useful to have an automatic way to make this chord change. Here are two ways to find a relative minor chord:

- **You can play a barred chord's relative minor by playing the first and second strings (or second and fourth strings) five frets above the barre.**

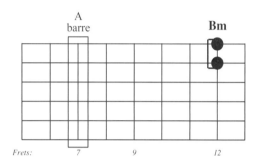

- **You can play a barred chord's relative minor by playing the first and third (or third and fourth) strings three frets below the barre:**

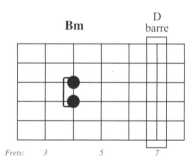

DO IT! (Regarding Minor Chords)

The following songs include many minor chords. Before playing each tune, take stock of which minor chords are needed, making sure that you know a few positions for each one.

WAYFARING STRANGER

TRACK 14

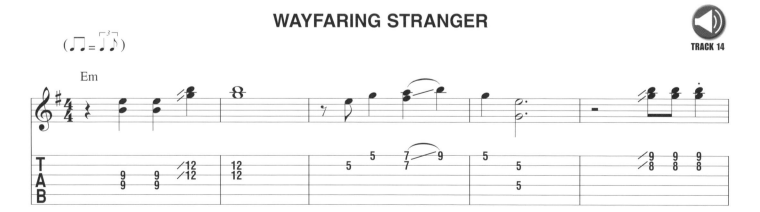

ST. JAMES INFIRMARY

G Tuning

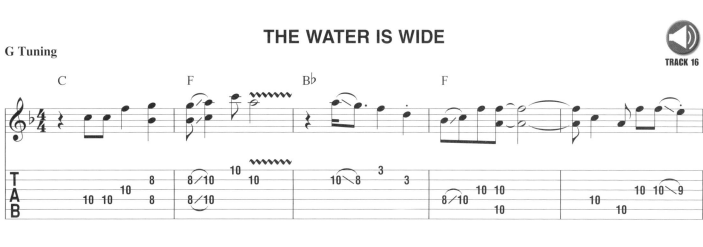

THE WATER IS WIDE

G Tuning

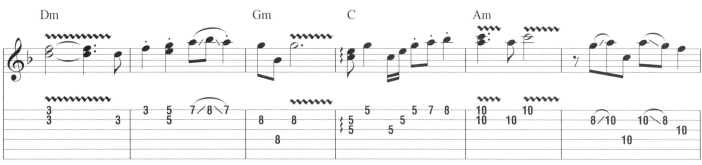

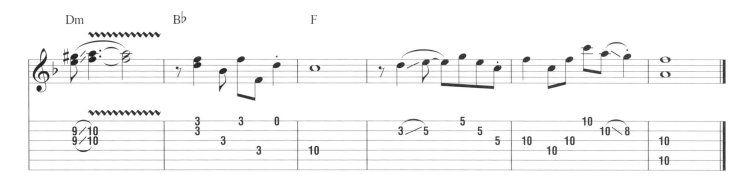

SCARBOROUGH FAIR

G Tuning

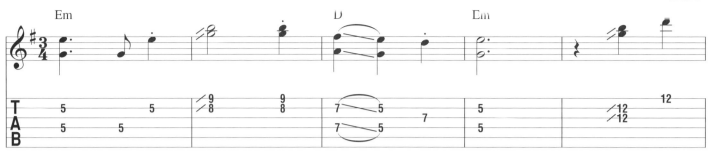

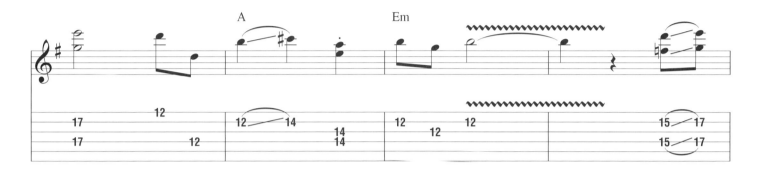

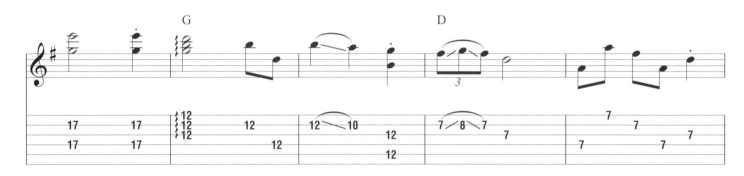

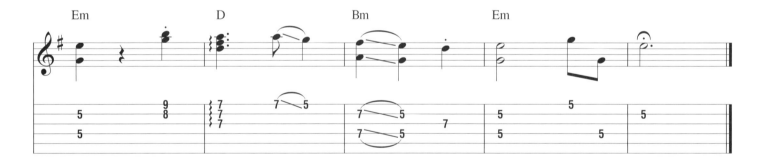

HOW? (Regarding the Second and Third Diagrams of ROADMAP #3)

Seventh chord: play the first and second (or second and fourth) strings three frets above the barre.

Ninth chord: play the second and third strings two frets below the barre.

Sixth chord: play the first and second (or second and fourth) strings five frets above the barre.

Diminished chord: play the first and second (or second and fourth) strings one fret below the barre. Since diminished chords repeat every three frets, you can play the same chord shape up or down three frets, six frets, or nine frets. (Diminished chords are written two ways: Cdim or C°.)

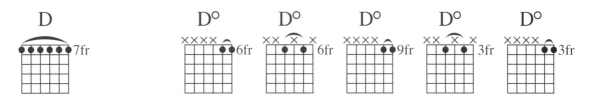

Augmented chord: play the second and third strings at the barre. Because augmented chords repeat every four frets, you can move this shape around, as you did with the diminished chord shape, and you can play "whole-step licks," as shown below. (Augmented chords are written two ways: Caug or C+.)

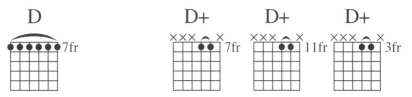

G Tuning

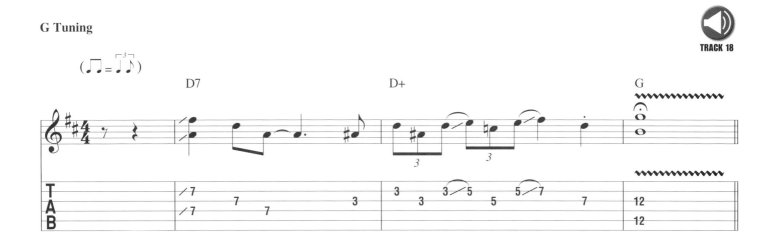

You can also play an augmented chord by playing a slant on the first and second strings at the barre:

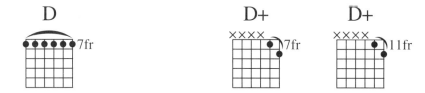

Major chord with tonic (root) on the first string: play a slant chord on the first and third strings, five frets above the barre. In country music, this is often used in an ending lick:

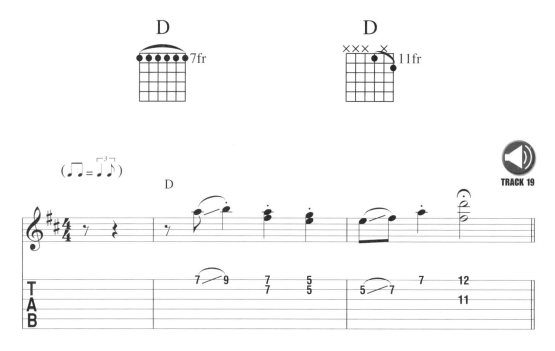

IV chord (major): play a slant chord on the first and second strings, one fret above the barre. You can move this chord up two frets to play the V chord.

IV chord (ninth): play a slant on the first and second strings, one fret below the barre. You can move this chord up two frets to play the V chord.

V chord (tonic on first string): play a slant on the first and third strings, one fret below the barre. You can move this shape down two frets to play the IV chord.

V chord (seventh): play the first and second (or second and fourth) strings two frets below the barre. You can move this shape down two frets to play the IV chord.

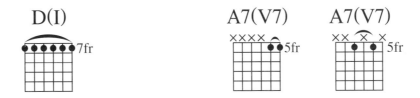

DO IT! (Regarding the Second and Third Diagrams of ROADMAP #3)

The following backup and solos for two old folk blues make use of many of the above chord shapes. Notice how the sixths and ninths give "Corrine, Corrina" a swing sound. (Chords in parentheses are played by the steel guitar, not the rhythm guitar.)

CORRINE, CORRINA

TRACK 20

G Tuning

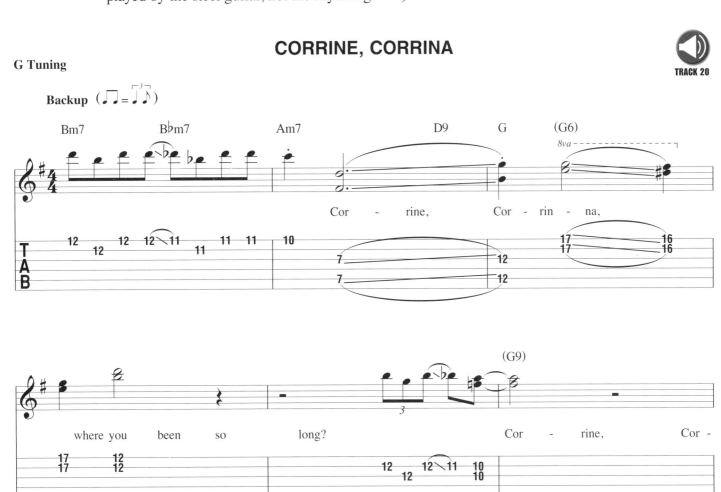

rin-na,   where you been so long?   Ain't had no

lovin'   since you've been gone.

"Tain't Nobody's Biz-ness If I Do" was popularized by Bessie Smith in the '20s and has become a blues/jazz standard. It has pop/ragtimey chord changes:

TAIN'T NOBODY'S BIZ-NESS IF I DO

This rock/ballad, which has a common pop progression, makes use of many chord shapes discussed in this chapter.

TURN AROUND

TRACK 22

G Tuning

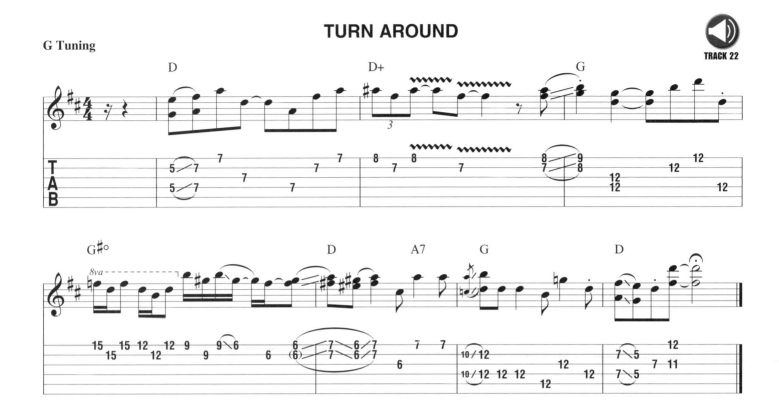

SUMMING UP—NOW YOU KNOW...

1. Several ways to play minor chords in G tuning
2. How to find any major chord's relative minor
3. How to play sixth, seventh, ninth, diminished, and augmented chords
4. How to play several IV and V chords relative to a barred major chord
5. How to play some slant chords

THE G/D CONVERSION

G Tuning

G Major Scale

D Tuning

D Major Scale

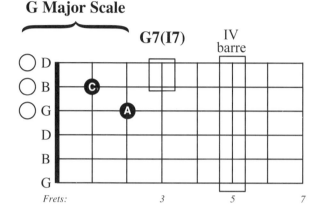

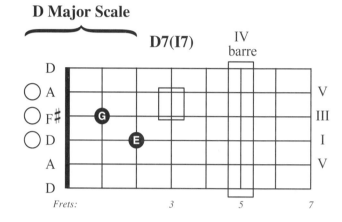

Both Tunings

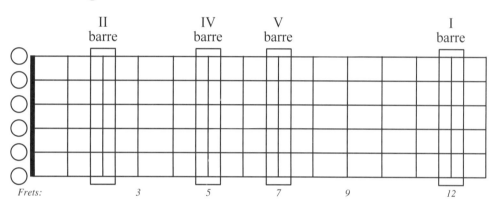

WHY? Before embarking on D tuning ("Oh no! A new tuning! I have to relearn everything!"), you'll be happy to know that there's a relationship between the G and D tunings that makes it possible for you to borrow licks or solos from one tuning and use them in the other. You're not starting from square one!

WHAT? In D tuning, you can use G licks, scales, solos, and chords if you move them down one string set. A G-tuning lick that is played on the first string can be played in D tuning on the second string. A melody played on the second and third strings in G tuning can be played on the third and fourth strings in D tuning. That's because the string-to-string intervals on the top four strings (1–4) in G tuning match the string-to-string intervals on the middle four strings (2–5) in D tuning.

G-TUNING INTERVALS	D-TUNING INTERVALS
First string = 5th	5th = Second string
Second string = 3rd	3rd = Third string
Third string = Root	Root = Fourth string
Fourth string = 5th	5th = Fifth string

Conversely, you can steal any D-tuning licks, scales, solos, or chords and use them in G tuning by moving them up one string set. Any D-tuning lick or chord that doesn't use the first string is eligible for this conversion.

HOW? D tuning is **D–A–D–F♯–A–D.** To get to D tuning from G tuning, leave the fourth and first strings at D, then:

- Tune the sixth string down to D (two-and-a-half steps/five frets).
- Tune the fifth string down to A (one whole step/two frets).
- Tune the third string down to F♯ (one half step/one fret).
- Tune the second strind down to A (one whole step/two frets).

When in D tuning, "convert" a G-tuning lick by playing first-string notes on the second string, second-string notes on the third string, and so on. Here's a G-tuning "turnaround" converted to D tuning. Note that chords, as well as licks, are moved down a string. (A *turnaround* is a lick that ends an eight- or 12-bar phrase in a blues tune.)

G Tuning

D Tuning

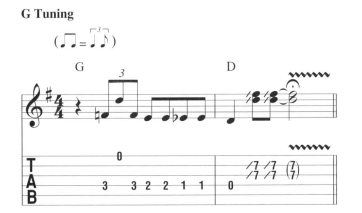

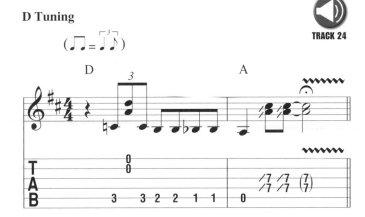

When in G tuning, "convert" a D-tuning lick by playing it one string higher, as this turnaround illustrates:

D Tuning

G Tuning

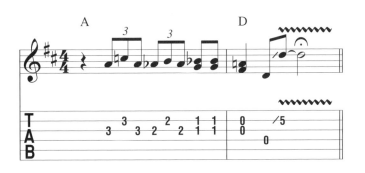

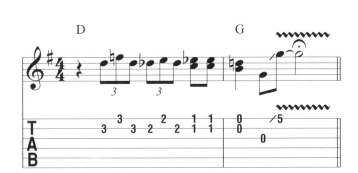

36

DO IT! Here's "Chilly Winds" in D tuning, transposed from the G tuning version in the **ROADMAP #1** chapter. It's the exact same solo, just moved down a string set.

CHILLY WINDS II

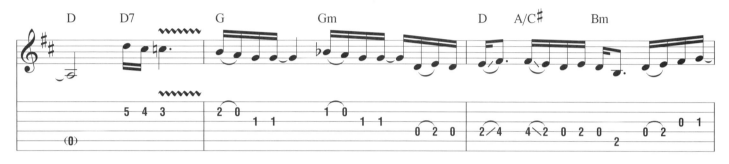

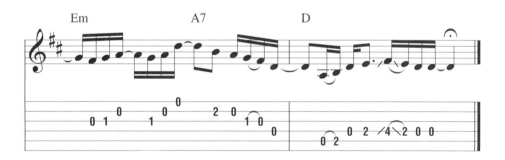

SUMMING UP—NOW YOU KNOW...

1. How to convert G-tuning licks and solos to D tuning

2. How to convert D-tuning licks and solos to G tuning

D TUNING: FIRST POSITION

Blues Scale   **Major Scale**

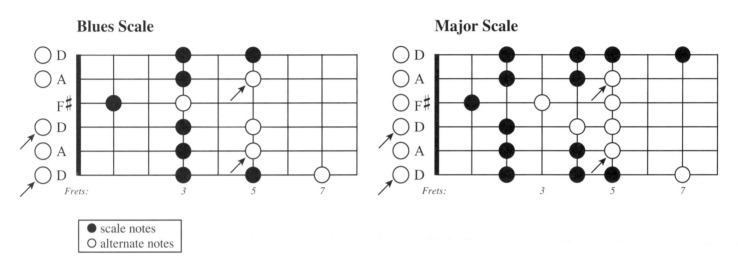

● scale notes
○ alternate notes

WHY? This popular open tuning is useful for blues, country, and rock. Slide guitarists Elmore James and "Blind" Willie Johnson used it, as do blues/rock players like Ry Cooder and Dave Lindley.

WHAT? **The diagrams of ROADMAP #5 show the first-position major and blues scales for open D tuning.** When you strum the open strings in this tuning, you play a D major chord.

As with the G-tuning scales, the D-tuning scales are guidelines. Sometimes other notes (between the notes indicated above) work.

The arrows point out the tonic (D) notes. In this tuning, there's an open high tonic note (D) on the first string.

The white dots are "alternates." They are duplicated by open strings or by higher strings. For example, the second string/fifth fret and the open first string are both D.

HOW? **Tune to open D (D–A–D–F♯–A–D), as shown in the previous chapter.**

Play the scales, ascending and descending.

D Tuning

D Blues Scale

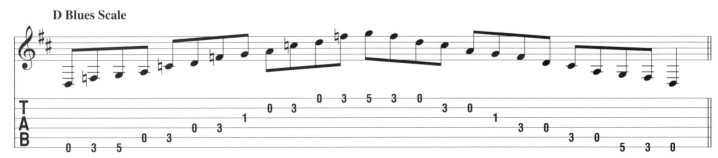

D Tuning

D Major Scale

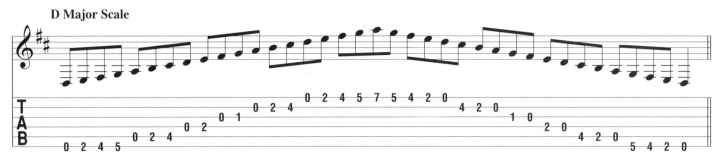

DO IT! **Use the blues scale to ad-lib solos throughout a bluesy tune.** Here's "Blues Traveler" in the key of D, in D tuning. All of the soloing is based on the D blues scale.

BLUES TRAVELER

D Tuning

TRACK 26

Use the blues scale to play melody and blues licks. In the following solo, the steel plays the melody and fills to "See, See Rider" in the key of D (in D tuning).

SEE, SEE RIDER III

D Tuning

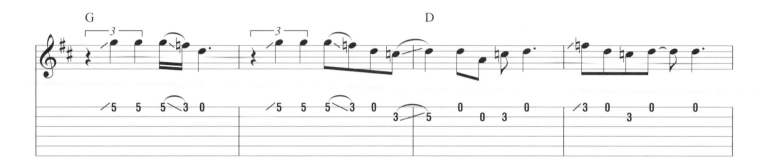

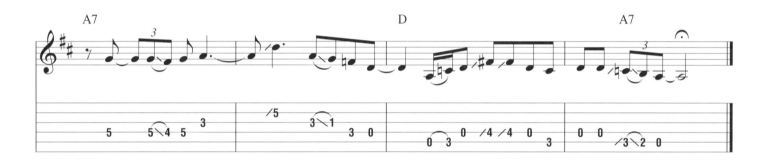

Use the major scale to play melodies and ad-lib solos. In "Streets of Laredo" (below), the melody and fills are based on the major scale.

STREETS OF LAREDO

G Tuning

You can use many of your **D-tuning licks and solos in G tuning,** as mentioned in the previous chapter. Here's "Streets of Laredo" in G tuning, transposed from the D-tuning version. The arrangement is moved up a string set to accommodate the G tuning, and the second half of the tune, which was played mostly on the first string in D tuning, is therefore not included.

STREETS OF LAREDO

G Tuning

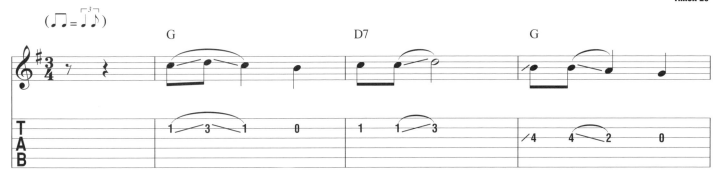

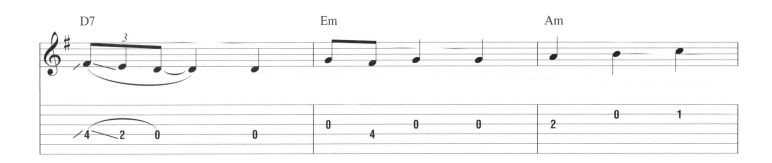

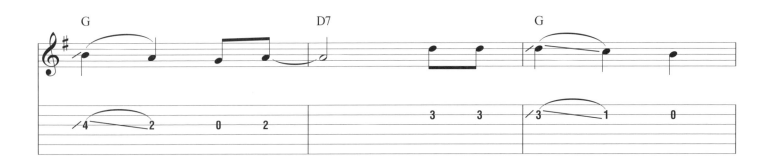

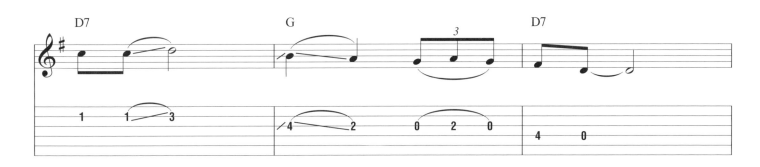

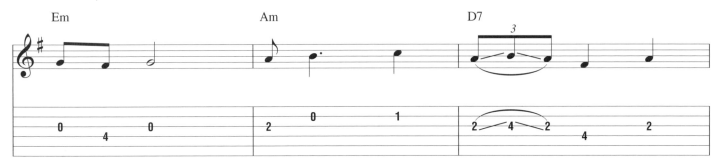

SUMMING UP—NOW YOU KNOW...

1. How to tune to open D
2. How to play a first-position D blues scale
3. How to play a first-position D major scale
4. How to use both scales to play melodies and ad-lib solos and licks
5. How to convert D-tuning arrangements to G tuning

D TUNING: SOLOING UP THE NECK

D Blues Scale

D Major Scale

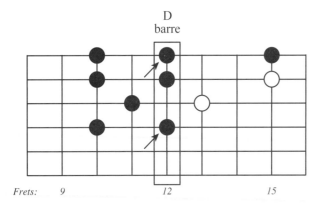

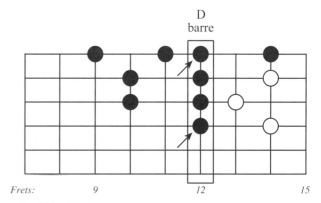

- ● scale notes
- ○ alternate notes

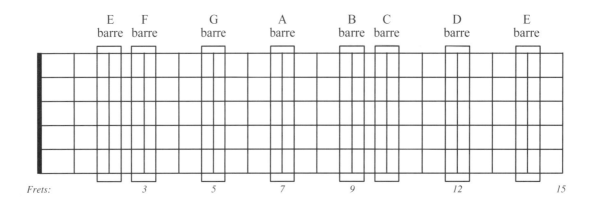

WHY? The scales and chords in **ROADMAP #6** make it possible to solo and ad-lib licks in any key, in D tuning.

WHAT? **The above diagrams show two moveable scales: D major and D blues.** Both scales have the same "home base": the barred D chord at the 12th fret. The arrows point out the tonic (D) notes.

The white dots are "alternates"—notes that are duplicated by higher strings (e.g., the third string/13th fret and the second string/10th fret are both G notes.)

The "inside 4" strings (5–2) have the same scale configurations as the "top 4" strings (4–1) in G tuning. Therefore, you already know most of the moveable major scale in D tuning.

ROADMAP #6 (the lower diagram) shows where all the barred major chords are located. You can base solos and backup on chords, just as you did in G tuning.

As in G tuning, the "sharp" and "flat" major chords are found between the indicated chords, and the fretboard "starts over" at the 12th fret. The D barre at the 12th fret matches the open-string D chord; the 14th-fret E chord matches the 2nd-fret E, and so on.

HOW? Play the scales, ascending and descending.

D Tuning

D Blues Scale

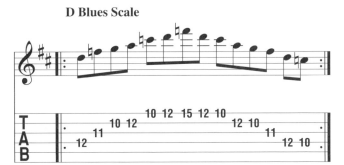

D Tuning

D Major Scale

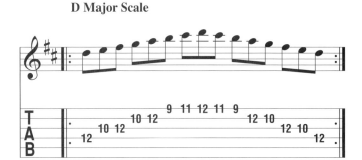

Study the barred chords in **ROADMAP #6** (the lower chart) and then play both moveable scales in other keys. Play the A major scale, the C blues scale, etc.

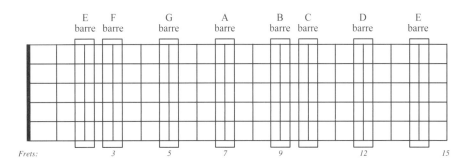

D Tuning

C Blues Scale

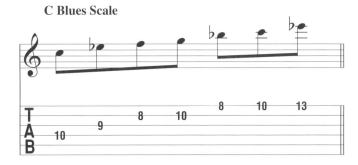

The principles that you learned in G tuning are true of D tuning (or any tuning), as well:

- **You can play chord-based licks and melodies by following a song's chord changes,** playing the appropriate barred chords.

- **Besides playing the notes of a barred chord, you can play major scale and blues scale notes** for each barre.

- **Before playing a song, make sure that you know where the I, IV, and V chords are located. The relationships on the fretboard are the same in both tunings (G and D):**
  - The IV chord is always five frets above the I chord.
  - The V chord is always two frets above the IV chord (seven frets above the I chord), or five frets below the I chord.

- **Find other chords (II, ♭VII, VI, etc.) by relating them to the I, IV, and V.** The II chord is always two frets above the I chord, the ♭VII chord is always two frets below the I chord, and so on.

DO IT!

Use the moveable blues scale to ad-lib solos to bluesy tunes like "Elmore's Blues," which follows. The song is a tip of the hat to the great Elmore James, who used D tuning when playing bottleneck guitar.

ELMORE'S BLUES

Use the moveable major scale to play melodies and solos in keys other than D. Here's a melodic solo to "Amazing Grace" in the key of C (10th fret). It's very similar to the G-tuning version in the **ROADMAP #2** chapter:

AMAZING GRACE II

Use the moveable major scale to ad-lib backup licks to "Careless Love" in the key of E (14th fret). It's an old folk blues:

CARELESS LOVE

Play backup and melody to "Stagolee" in the key of E by following the song's chord changes:

STAGOLEE II

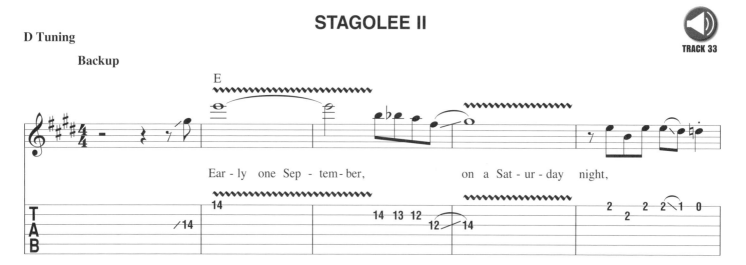

Stag - o - lee and Bil - ly De   Ly - ons   had a ter - ri - ble   fight.   He's a

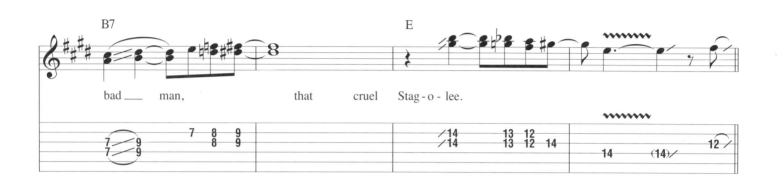

bad ___ man,   that   cruel   Stag - o - lee.

You can play the second and third notes of the major scale on the first string. These notes will come in handy in countless tunes. For example, "Stagolee II," above, could have begun like this:

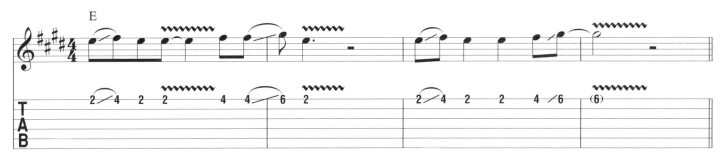

Here's a chord-based solo to "I Never Will Marry" in the key of G, in D tuning:

I NEVER WILL MARRY II

The solo to "Southern Rock," in the key of A, is chord-based:

SOUNTHERN ROCK

D Tuning

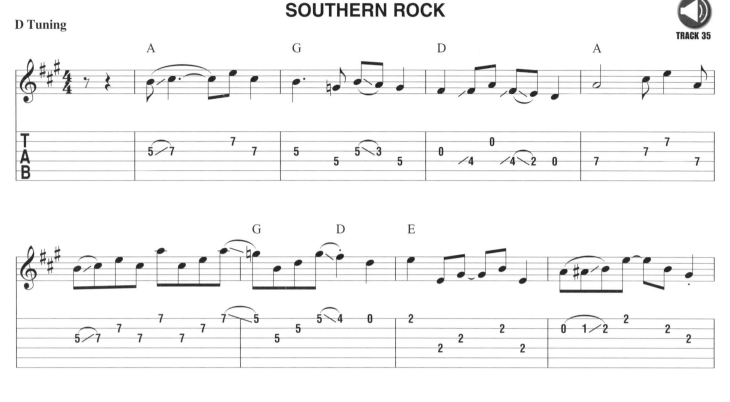

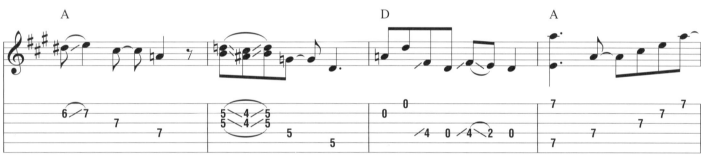

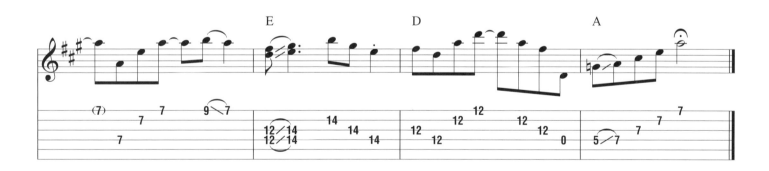

SUMMING UP—NOW YOU KNOW...

1. How to play a moveable blues scale in D tuning

2. How to play a moveable major scale in D tuning

3. How to use both scales to play solos and licks in any key

4. How to play all of the barred major chords in D tuning

5. How to play chord-based solos and backup in D tuning, in any key

D TUNING: SLANTS, MINORS, AND OTHER CHORDS

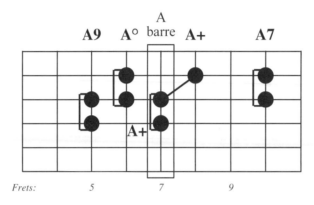

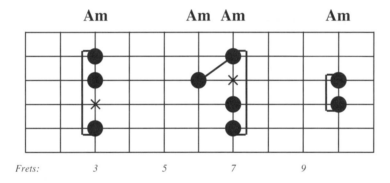

WHY? You can acquire a large chord vocabulary in D tuning by taking the chord ideas of **ROADMAP #3** and moving them up a string.

WHAT? **The above diagrams show how to find many A chords (A7, A9, etc.) by relating them to the barred A chord.** For example, there's an A7 on the second and third strings, three frets above the barred A chord.

ROADMAP #7 shows moveable chord relationships: For example, to play any seventh chord, play the second and third strings, three frets above the barred major chord.

All the chord shapes of ROADMAP #7 are moved up a string from the G-tuning chords. In G tuning, to play a ninth chord, you play the second and third strings two frets below the barred major chord. In D tuning, to play a ninth chord, you play the third and fourth strings two frets below the barred major chord.

HOW?   Here are some examples of G tuning-to-D tuning chord conversions:

- You can make any barred major chord into a minor chord by slanting back on the third string.

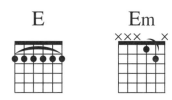

- Seventh chord: play the second and third (or third and fifth) strings three frets above the barre.

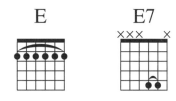

- Ninth chord: play the third and fourth strings two frets below the barre.

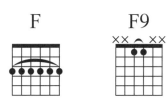

- Diminished chord: play the second and third (or third and fifth) strings one fret below the barre.

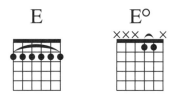

- Augmented chord: play a slant chord with the third string at the barre and the second string one fret above the barre.

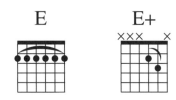

DO IT! Play the following tunes, which have been converted to D tuning from the G tuning versions in previous chapters:

WAYFARING STRANGER II

TRACK 36

D Tuning

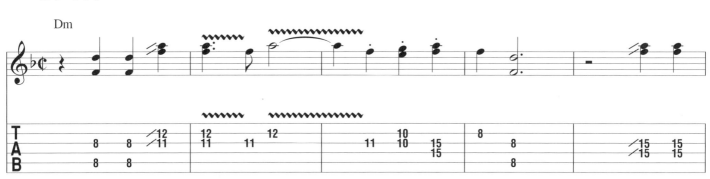

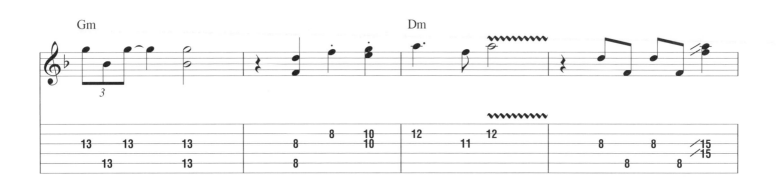

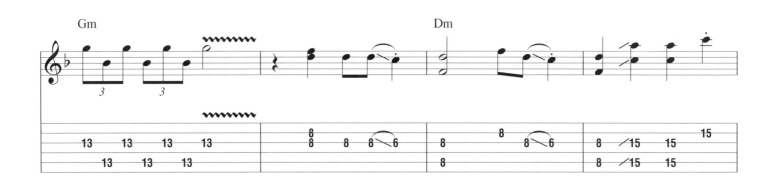

54

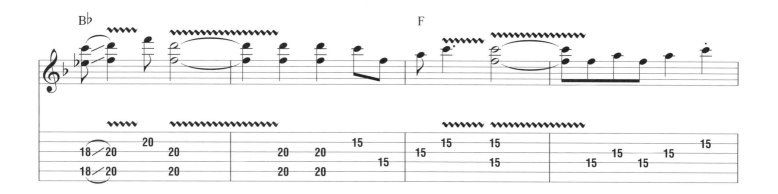

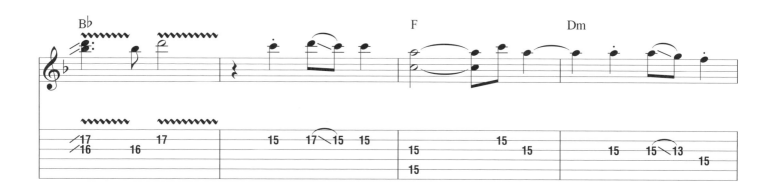

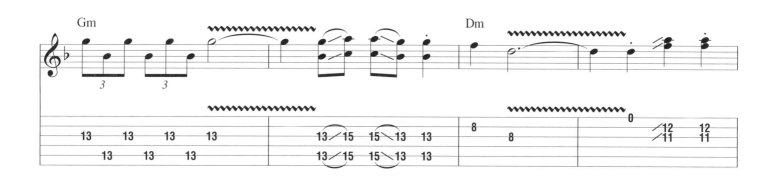

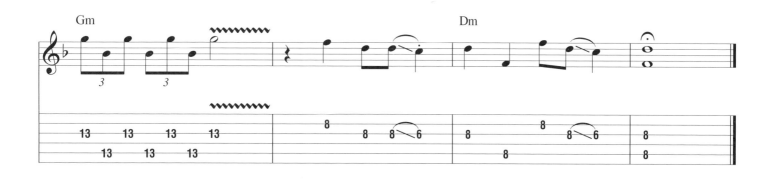

D Tuning

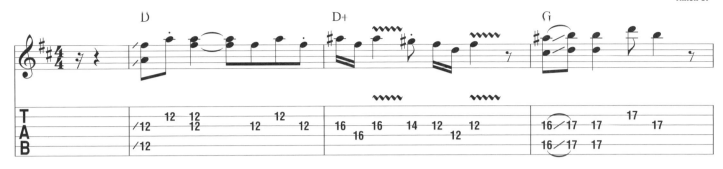

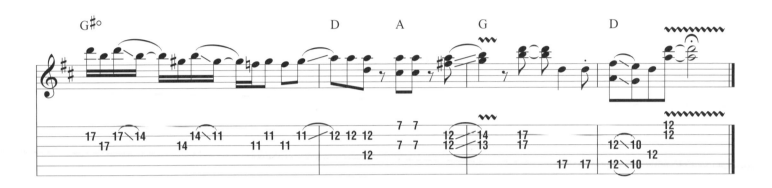

SUMMING UP—NOW YOU KNOW...

1. How to play minor, ninth, seventh, sixth, diminished, and augmented chords by converting G-tuning chord shapes to D tuning

2. How to play some slant chords in D tuning

E7 TUNING: CHORDS AND SCALES

Chords: E(V)   A(I) E7(V7)   A(I)

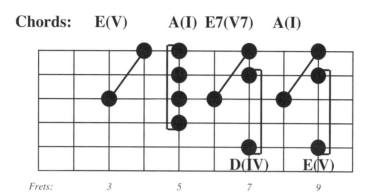

D(IV)   E(V)

Frets: 3   5   7   9

A Major Scale

IV   VIII V   VI   VII

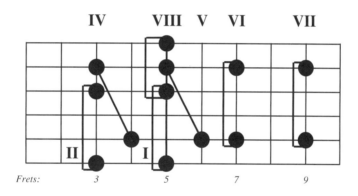

II   I

Frets: 3   5   7   9

A Major Scale

I   II   III   IV

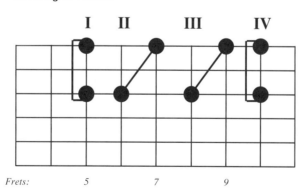

Frets: 5   7   9

WHY?   Many early lap-steel books taught this popular tuning, and it is still widely used by six-string players. E7 tuning is used to play classic country, blues, pretty ballads, and jazzy tunes.

WHAT? Unlike the major chord of G tuning and D tuning, a strum across the open strings in E7 tuning gives you a seventh chord: E7.

The good news: E7 tuning is very similar to D tuning. The intervals of the top four strings are the same, so you can use many licks, scales, and chords from the D tuning roadmaps, as long as you adjust everything up a whole step. For example, a D-tuning D chord becomes an E7-tuning E chord (on the top four strings); a G becomes an A, and so on.

In terms of intervals, the sixth and fifth strings of E7 tuning differ from D-tuning intervals. In E7 tuning, the open strings form an E7 chord: the sixth string is a V (B) and the fifth string is a ♭VII (D).

Barred chords are seventh chords in E7 tuning—if you include the fifth string.

Seventh chords have several uses and E7 tuning is handy for all of them:

- In many blues tunes, all three chords (I, IV, and V) are sevenths. It's one of the factors that creates a bluesy sound.

- In non-blues music (pop, country, jazz, etc.), seventh chords "lead up a 4th." When you play an E7, it makes you want to hear an A chord (a 4th above E7); G7 leads to C, and so on. (Play some seventh chords, then play the major chord that's a 4th higher, and feel the tension and resolution.)

- Many songs have circle-of-5ths-type chord changes in which you leave the chord family and go to the VI, III, or ♭VII chord, then move in 4ths, playing seventh chords, to return to the I chord. The blues/bluegrass tune "Salty Dog" is an example of this type of progression: G–E7–A7–D7–G. E7 tuning makes it easy to play all of those seventh chords. (For more on circle-of-5ths progressions, see *Fretboard Roadmaps for Guitar [Second Edition]* or *Fretboard Roadmaps for Jazz Guitar*).

- The top diagram of **ROADMAP #8** shows several partial chords and how they relate to a barred chord. For example, the second and fifth strings, played two frets above a barre, form a partial IV chord. All the relationships shown in this roadmap are moveable.

The lower diagrams of ROADMAP #8 show two ways to play an A major scale. The first way involves the use of *backward slants* in which a lower string is fretted one fret above a higher string. Both major scales are "harmonized"; in this case, the upper note is the major scale, while the lower note is a harmony note. (When you use major scales to play melodies, the harmony notes give you a richer, prettier sound.)

The roman numerals represent scale intervals.

HOW? Here's the tuning, from the sixth to the first string: B–D–E–G♯–B–E:

TRACK 38

Tune the sixth string to B.

Tune the fifth string to D.

Tune the fourth string to E

Tune the third string to G♯.

Tune the second string to B.

Tune the first string to E.

All of the D-tuning chords described in ROADMAP #7 are applicable to E7 tuning, as long as you adjust everything up a whole step (D7 in D tuning becomes E7 in E7 tuning) and don't include the fifth string—that goes for minor, ninth, diminished, and augmented chords. Here's **ROADMAP #7** adjusted to E7 tuning:

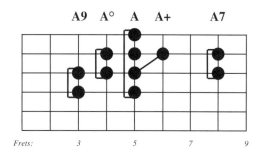

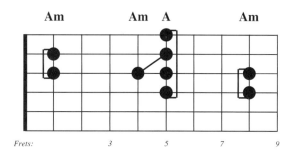

The first, third, and fourth strings of the major barre also form its (partial) relative minor:

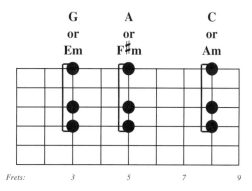

The second and fifth strings, played two frets above the barre, form a partial major chord a 4th above the barre (the IV chord). Raise that shape two frets for the V chord:

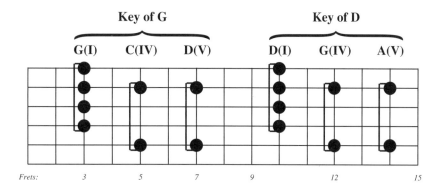

59

A forward slant chord on the first and third strings, one fret above the barre, forms a partial V7 chord of the barre. Raise it two frets for a higher I chord:

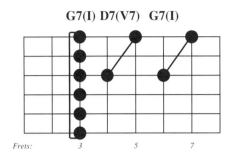

G7(I) D7(V7) G7(I)

Frets: 3   5   7

A forward slant chord on the first and third strings, one fret below a barre, forms the V chord of the barre:

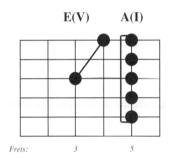

E(V)   A(I)

Frets: 3   5

Here are two major scales, as shown in the bottom two diagrams of **ROADMAP #8**. The right-hand fretboard roadmap shows a partial A major scale that starts where the left-hand roadmap leaves off:

A Major Scale

A Major Scale

These scales are moveable. Play the A major scale two frets higher and it becomes B major.

Here are all of the barred chords, up and down the fretboard, in E7 tuning. They're all seventh chords, but if you omit the fifth string, they become major chords:

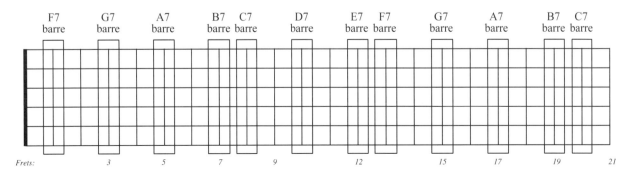

| F7 barre | G7 barre | A7 barre | B7 barre | C7 barre | D7 barre | E7 barre | F7 barre | G7 barre | A7 barre | B7 barre | C7 barre |

Frets: 3   5   7   9   12   15   17   19   21

60

DO IT! The following songs make use of the scale and chord shapes of **ROADMAP #8**.

"The Great Speckled Bird," below, is an old country gospel tune with a melody and chord progression similar to many popular country tunes (e.g., "I'm Thinking Tonight of My Blue Eyes," "Wild Side of Life," and "The Prisoner's Song"). In the key of E, it has the usual three chords: I, IV, and V. The E7 tuning makes it easy to enhance the progression with E7 and B7 chords.

THE GREAT SPECKLED BIRD

E7 Tuning

TRACK 39

This key-of-A version of "Careless Love" uses two A chords (at the fifth and 17th frets), an E7 at the 12th fret, and a D at the 10th fret.

CARELESS LOVE II

"Beautiful Brown Eyes" is an old country/folk tune. The arrangement below gives you a slant-chord workout. This three-chord song consists of G (at the third fret), C (eighth fret), and D (10th fret) and some harmonized scale movement:

BEATIFUL BROWN EYES

When Arlo Guthrie wrote "Alice's Restaurant," he based it on a chord progression that was well-known to fans of the blues and early swing music. Songs like "Bring It on Down to My House, Honey" and "They're Red Hot," and a host of other bawdy blues, share nearly the same chord progression. Since it involves circle-of-5ths chord movement, the progression is easy to play in E7 tuning. "Six to Five," below, is typical of this genre:

SIX TO FIVE

"Betty and Dupree," an old folk tune, has a typical 12-bar blues format and uses seventh chords throughout:

BETTY AND DUPREE

"Blues Riff," below, makes effective use of seventh chords:

BLUES RIFF

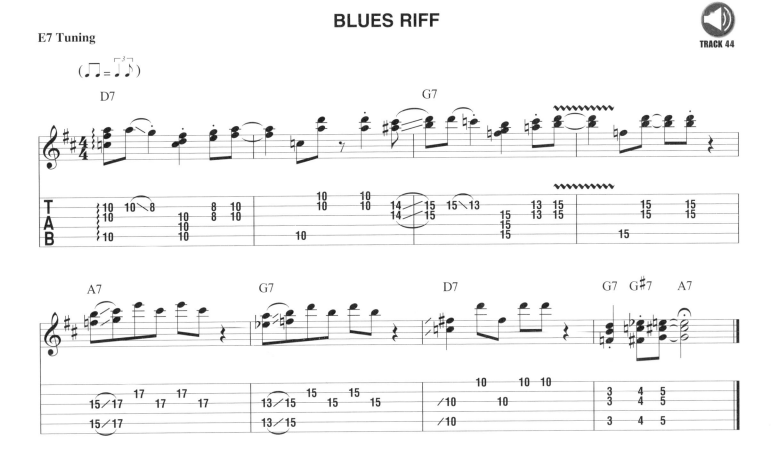

E7 Tuning

Dating back to the Civil War, "Aura Lee" is the American song on which Elvis Presley's "Love Me Tender" is based. It's a beautiful ballad that includes several seventh chords, as well as minor chords:

AURA LEE

E7 Tuning

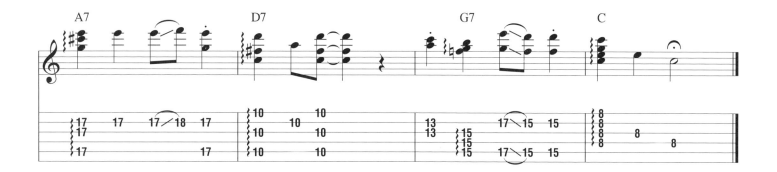

SUMMING UP—NOW YOU KNOW...

1. How to tune to E7

2. How to convert D-tuning chords to E7-tuning chords

3. How to play barred major and seventh chords all over the fretboard

4. How to play many partial chords (minors, sevenths, IV and V chords, etc.) in relation to a barred chord

5. Two ways to play a major scale in E7 tuning

C6 TUNING: CHORDS AND A SCALE

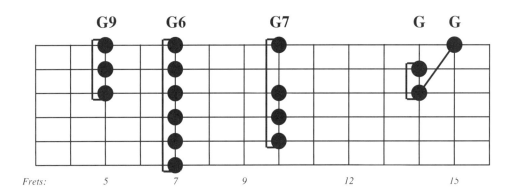

G Major Scale

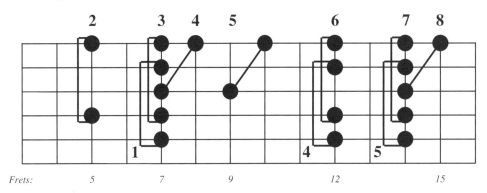

WHY? C6 is one of the most popular lap-steel tunings for Hawaiian music and retro country. The steel players who accompanied Hank Williams, Hank Thompson, and other stars of the late '40s and '50s often played in C6, so modern steel players use the tuning to evoke those classic country sounds.

WHAT? **The upper diagram shows how to find many G chords (G, G6, G7, and G9) by relating them to the barred G6 chord.** For example, G7 is played on the first and fourth strings (third and fifth are optional), three frets above the barred G6 chord.

All of the G chord variations are moveable—they apply to any barred chord. For example, to play any seventh chord, play the first and fourth strings, three frets above the barred major chord.

The lower diagram shows how to play a harmonized G major scale, using pairs of notes. The lower note of each pair is a harmony note. The numbers represent the degrees of the major scale.

There are two ways to play the fourth and fifth scale degrees: you can use slant chords or "straight" chords.

This major scale is moveable. If you play the same scale two frets higher (starting with the barred A6 chord at the ninth fret), it's an A major scale.

HOW?

Here's the C6 tuning: C–E–G–A–C–E. It's a C major chord with an A note, which is the sixth note of the C major scale. When you strum the open strings, you'll hear a C6 chord:

TRACK 46

Tune the sixth string to C.

Tune the fifth string to E.

Tune the fourth string to G.

Tune the third string to A.

Tune the second string to C.

Tune the first string to E.

C6 tuning is not completely unrelated to G tuning; in fact, it has some similarities. Look at the intervals of each tuning:

	G TUNING	C6 TUNING
Sixth string	Root	Root
Fifth string	3rd	3rd
Fourth string	5th	5th
Third string	Root	6th
Second string	3rd	Root
First string	5th	3rd

Notice that the lower three strings of G tuning (strings 6–4) have the same intervals as the lower three strings of the C6 tuning. Also, the lower five strings of G tuning (strings 6–2) have the same intervals as the C6 tuning, if you ignore the A note/3rd string in C6. You can duplicate many G tuning licks by making this adjustment.

G Tuning   C6 Tuning

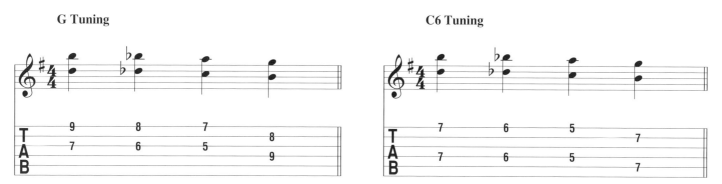

Play the G major scale in C6 tuning, ascending and descending:

TRACK 47

C6 Tuning

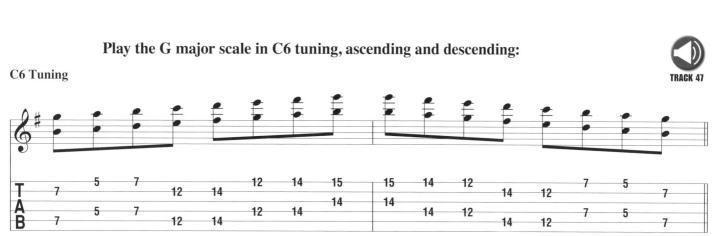

Here's the same scale, using the alternate 4th and 5th intervals (the slant chords):

C6 Tuning

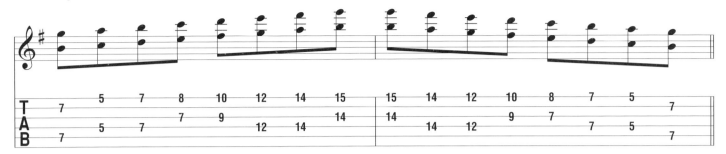

The diagram below shows all of the barred sixth chords, except for the "sharps" and "flats":

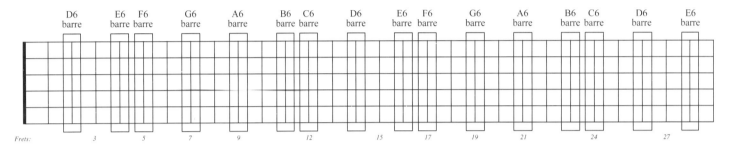

As in G and D tunings, or any open tuning, the IV chord is always five frets above the I chord, and the V chord is always two frets higher than the IV chord.

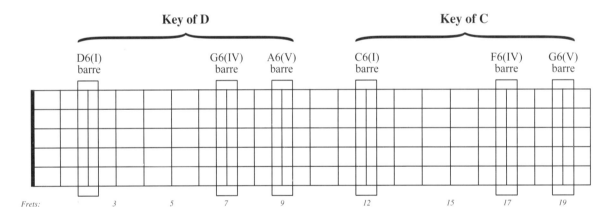

As shown in ROADMAP #9, G9 is played on the first, second, and third strings, two frets below the barre. This is a moveable relationship:

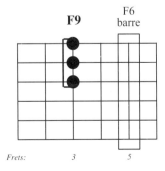
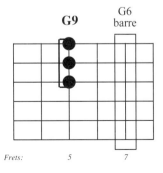
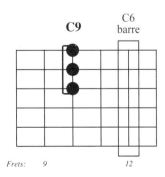

Also shown in **ROADMAP #9**, G7 is played on the first, third, fourth, and fifth strings, three frets above the barre. This is another moveable relationship:

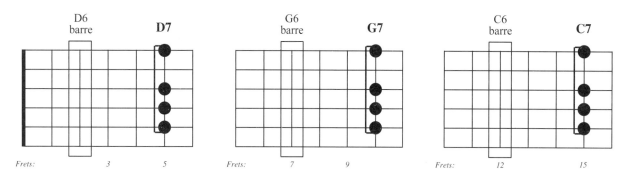

The barred G6 chord (at the seventh fret) has a high B (the 3rd of the G6 chord) on the first string. This is true of all barred chords: the first string is the 3rd of the chord. When you play a barred C6 at the 12th fret, the first string is E, the 3rd interval in a C chord.

If you want a major chord with the interval of the 5th on top, play the second and third strings, seven frets above the barre. In **ROADMAP #9**, the G6 barre is located at the seventh fret. If you play the second and third strings at the 14th fret, you'll be playing a partial G chord with D (the 5th) on top. This is true of all barred chords:

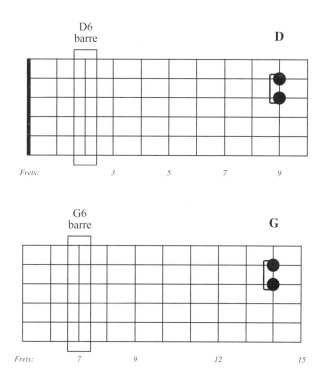

Raise the above two-note major chord three frets to play another seventh chord. Like all of the chord relationships in this chapter, this one is moveable:

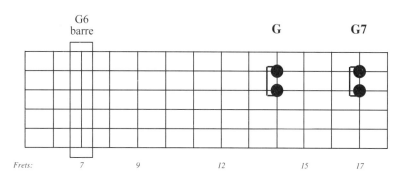

If you want a major chord with the root note on top, play a slant chord seven and eight frets (low to high) above the barre, as shown below:

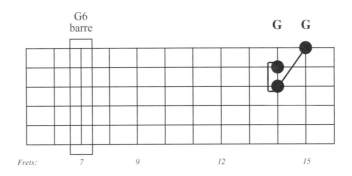

DO IT! Play the following tunes, which make use of the major scale and all of the chord (and partial chord) positions described in the "HOW?" section:

The following arrangement of "Beautiful Brown Eyes" shows how to transfer some of your G-tuning licks to C6 tuning. It uses barred chords almost exclusively, as well as the major scale diagrammed in **ROADMAP #9**: It's in the key of C, so your barred chords are C (12th fret), F (17th fret), and G (19th fret).

BEAUTIFUL BROWN EYES II

TRACK 48

C6 Tuning

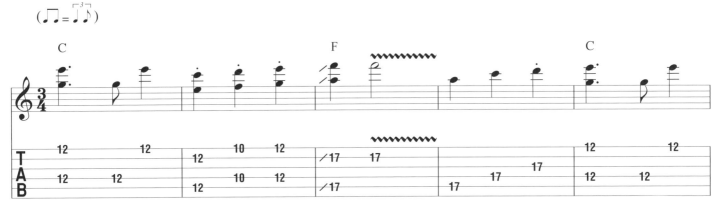

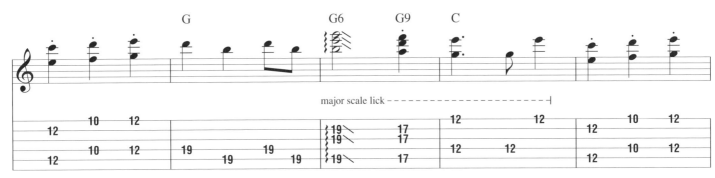

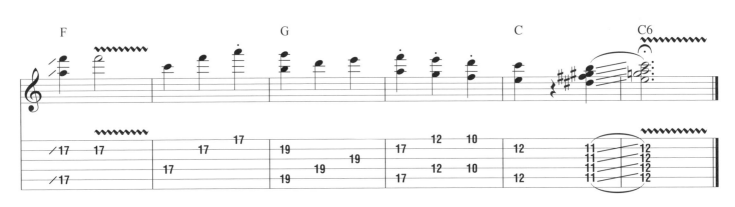

72

"Aloha Oe," the most famous Hawaiian song of all time, shows how effectively the C6 tuning evokes those swaying palm trees! This arrangement is in the key of G, so the barred chords are G (seventh fret), C (12th fret), and D (second fret). Notice the use of the D7 chord at the fifth fret and the high G6 chord (19th fret) that ends the tune. It's a classic Hawaiian ending: slide up to the I chord an octave higher than you were playing in the rest of the solo.

ALOHA OE

TRACK 49

In the key of A, the old cowboy song "Red River Valley" includes three barred chords: A (ninth fret), D (14th fret), and E (fourth and 16th frets), as well as a partial A chord at the 16th fret (twice). Note the slant chord in the final measure, which makes for a classic country ending.

RED RIVER VALLEY II

C6 Tuning

"Corrine, Corrina," also in A, benefits from the jazzy/bluesy sixth and ninth chords that are easy to play in C6 tuning.

CORRINE, CORRINA II

C6 Tuning

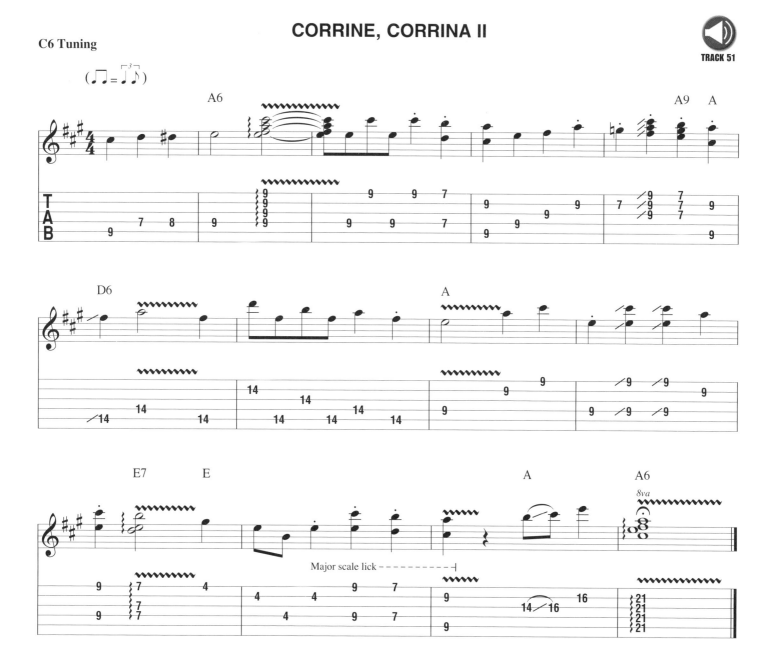

SUMMING UP—NOW YOU KNOW...

1. How to tune to C6

2. How to play barred chords all over the fretboard in C6 tuning

3. How to play many partial (two- or three-note) chords in relation to barred chords

4. Two ways to play a major scale, starting at the barred position, with a lower harmony note

C6 TUNING: MORE CHORDS

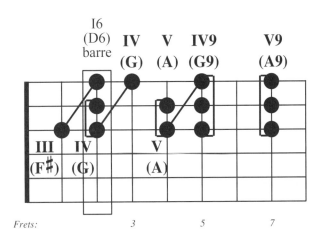

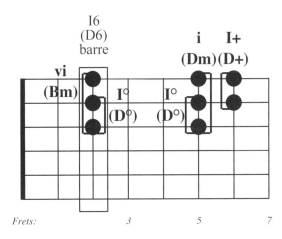

WHY? **ROADMAP #10** shows how to find more chords and partial chords (IV chords, V chords, minors, etc.) in relation to a barred chord. A bigger chord vocabulary makes it easier to play solos and accompaniment.

WHAT? While **ROADMAP #9** showed how to find variations of a barred chord, **ROADMAP #10** helps you find other chords (the IV chord, the V chord, the relative minor, etc.) in relation to a barre.

All of the chord relationships shown in **ROADMAP #10** are moveable. For example, to play a minor chord, play the first, second, and third strings three frets above a barred chord. A barre at the fifth fret is F6; the first, second, and third strings at the eighth fret form an Fm chord.

HOW? The diagrams above show two ways to locate a minor chord:

- **As mentioned above, play the top three strings three frets above the barre** (you can also include the fifth and sixth strings).

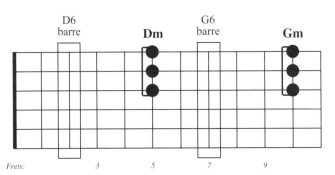

76

The top three strings of a barre chord form the relative minor of that barre (you can also include the fifth and sixth strings). For example, a barre at the 12th fret is C6; the top three strings at the 12th fret is Am, the relative minor of C.

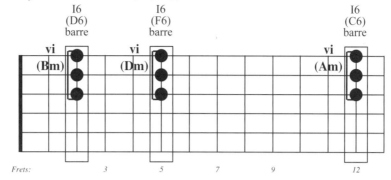

A slant chord with the third string at the barre and the first string one fret higher forms the IV chord of the barre. A slant chord two frets higher is the V chord:

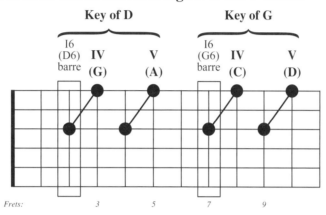

A slant chord with the third string one fret behind the barre and the first string at the barre forms the III chord:

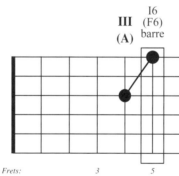

The second, third, and sixth strings at the barre form the IV chord. (The second and sixth strings are octaves, so the sixth string can always be played on the same fret as the second string. The same goes for the first and fifth strings.)

Key of D   Key of G

The second and third strings, three frets above this IV chord, form a IV7 chord. If you add the first string, it's a IV9 chord:

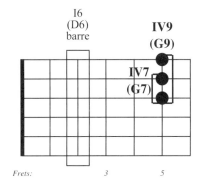

The second and third strings, two frets above the barre, form the V chord:

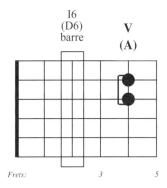

The second and third strings, three frets above this V chord, form a V7 chord. If you add the first string, it's a V9 chord:

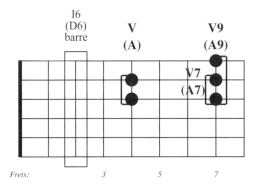

The second and third strings of a barred chord form a partial (two-note) diminished chord. Since diminished chords repeat every three frets, you can move that shape around:

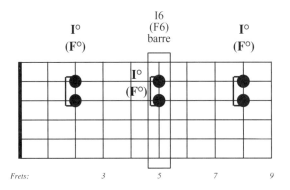

The first and second strings, four frets above a barred chord, form a partial augmented chord. Since augmented chords repeat every four frets, you can move that shape around. When you move the augmented shape up four frets, it's right below the IV chord. This is handy, as an augmented chord often resolves up a 4th:

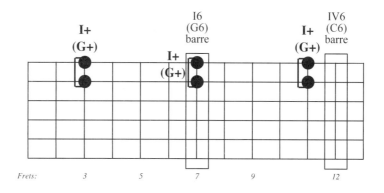

DO IT! Play the following tunes, which make use of the chords described above. In the slightly different version of "St. James Infirmary," below, notice how convenient the slant E chord is (it's located right next to the Am chord). This is good to remember, because it illustrates the relationship between a minor chord and its V chord.

ST. JAMES INFIRMARY II

C6 Tuning

TRACK 52

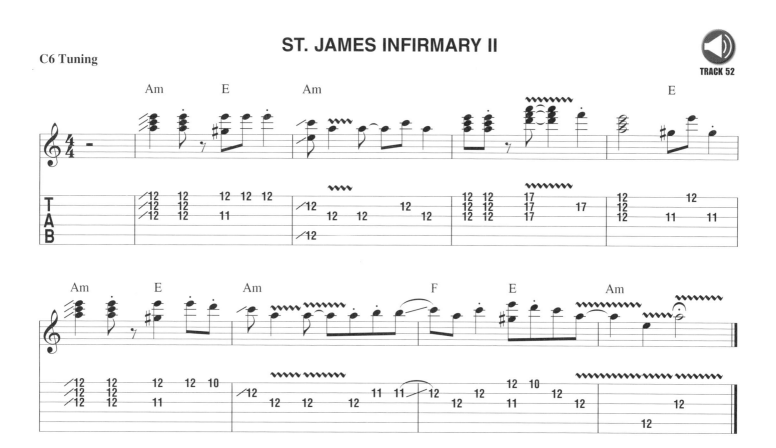

"The Water is Wide" has all three minor chords in the key of G: Em (the relative minor of the I chord, G), Am (the ii chord of the I chord and the relative minor of the IV chord, C), and Bm (the iii chord of the I chord and the relative minor of the V chord, D). Locate all six chords before playing the arrangement:

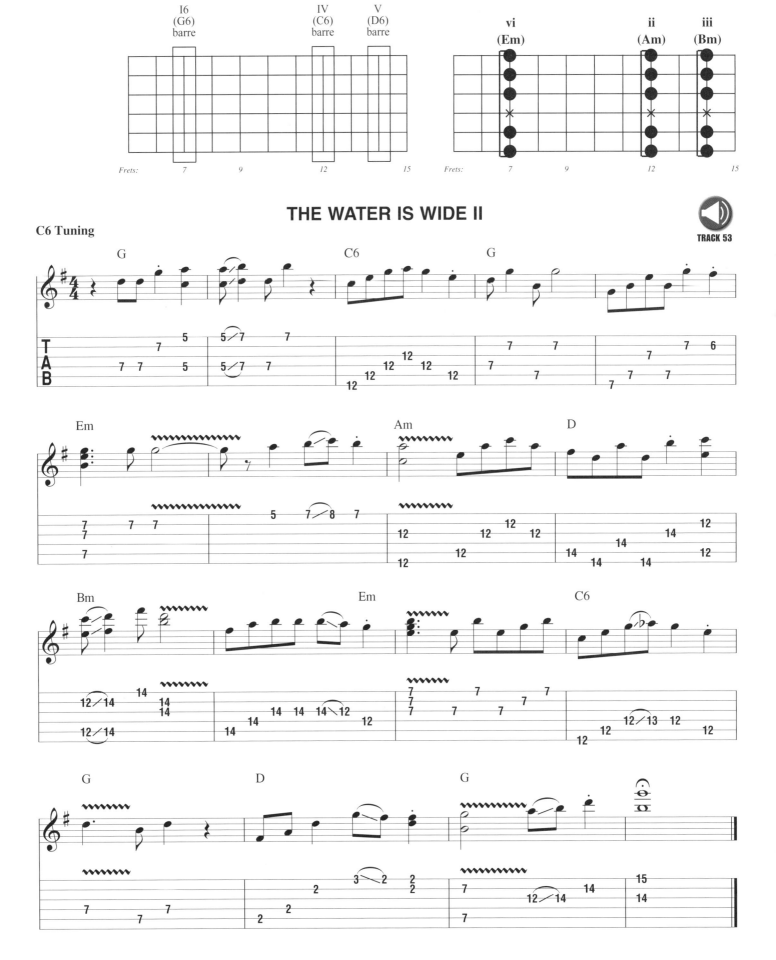

THE WATER IS WIDE II

TRACK 53

C6 Tuning

The following 12-bar blues includes jazzy chord substitutions and a swing feel. Note the ending: a classic jazz turnaround that includes both diminished and augmented chords.

TWELVE BAR SWING

Notice that measures 12–14 of "The Great Speckled Bird" nearly duplicate the melody of measures 4–6, but use different positions that don't require as much movement up the neck.

THE GREAT SPECKLED BIRD II

TRACK 55

C6 Tuning

This version of "Tain't Nobody's Biz-ness If I Do" makes use of sixth, ninth, and diminished chords and many of the positions diagrammed in **ROADMAP #10.**

TAIN'T NOBODY'S BIZ-NESS IF I DO

C6 Tuning

SUMMING UP—NOW YOU KNOW...

1. Two ways to play minor chords

2. How to find IV and V slant chords in relation to a barred chord

3. How to play many partial (two- and three-note) chords in relation to barred chords, including IV7, IV9, V7, and V9, plus diminished and augmented chords

MORE CONVERSIONS

G Blues Scale

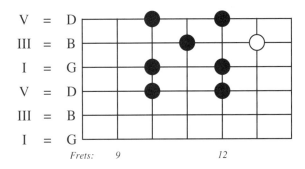

V	=	D
III	=	B
I	=	G
V	=	D
III	=	B
I	=	G

Frets: 9   12

A Blues Scale

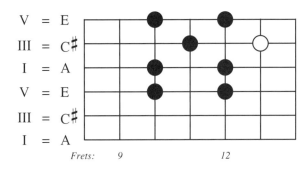

V	=	E
III	=	C♯
I	=	A
V	=	E
III	=	C♯
I	=	A

Frets: 9   12

D Blues Scale

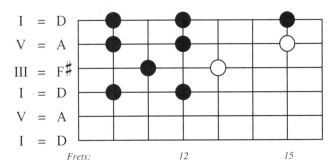

I	=	D
V	=	A
III	=	F♯
I	=	D
V	=	A
I	=	D

Frets: 12   15

E Blues Scale

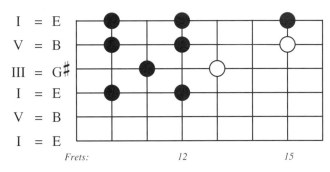

I	=	E
V	=	B
III	=	G♯
I	=	E
V	=	B
I	=	E

Frets: 12   15

WHY? There are many other lap-steel tunings. Some players like to tune to the key of the song that they're playing because they like to have an open tonic chord (I chord). Most of these tunings have a great deal in common with the tunings that you've learned so far: G, D, C6, and E7. Recognizing these similarities makes it easier to play in other tunings.

WHAT? **"Open A" tuning is the same as G tuning, only every string is tuned a whole step (two frets) higher.** Many of the early lap-steel books teach this tuning.

A similar A tuning features lower-pitched sixth and fifth strings. This is one of the oldest lap-steel tunings:

> 6th string = E
>
> 5th string = A
>
> 4th string = E
>
> 3rd string = A
>
> 2nd string = C♯
>
> 1st string = E

The open G tuning used by many Delta blues guitar players (Son House, Mississippi Fred McDowell, etc.) resembles this tuning, though it's dropped down a whole step.

"Open E" tuning is the same as D tuning, with every string tuned up a whole step (two frets).

"Open F" tuning is the same as G tuning, with every string tuned down a whole step (two frets); alternatively, you can use D tuning, with every string tuned up one-and-a-half steps (three frets).

You can tune to any open chord this way:

A♭	=	G tuning, up one half step (one fret)
A	=	G tuning, up one whole step (two frets)
B♭	=	G tuning, up one-and-a-half steps (three frets)
B	=	G tuning, up two whole steps (four frets), or D tuning, down one-and-a-half steps (three frets)
C	=	D tuning, down one whole step (two frets)
C♯	=	D tuning, down one half step (one fret)
E♭	=	D tuning, up one half step (one fret)
E	=	D tuning, up one whole step (two frets)
F	=	D tuning, up one-and-a-half steps (three frets), or G tuning, down one whole step (two frets)
G♭	=	G tuning, down one half step (one fret)

You can raise or lower the C6 tuning to play in D6, B♭6, and so on. You can also raise or lower E7 tuning to D7, F7, etc.

E13 tuning, also known as C♯m tuning, is the same as E7 tuning, but with the second string raised to C♯.

HOW?

When you play in any of these "converted" tunings, the chord shapes and relationships remain unchanged from the original tuning (the chord names change, however).

In "open A" tuning, all of the G-tuning chords and licks apply, but all of the chord names are a whole step (two frets) higher because A is a whole step above G.

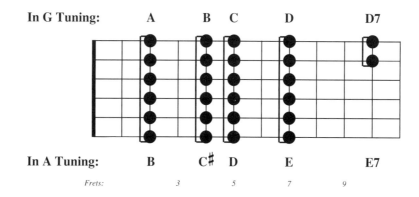

In "open C" tuning, the D-tuning chords and licks apply, but all of the chord names are a whole step (two frets) lower because C is a whole step below D.

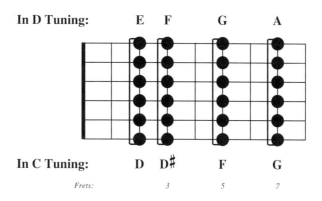

DO IT! Try playing some of the tunes in previous chapters in alternate tunings. Play the **ROADMAP #1** arrangement of "See See Rider" in A tuning (instead of G), or the **ROADMAP #6** arrangement of "Elmore's Blues" in E tuning (instead of D).

SUMMING UP—NOW YOU KNOW...

1. How to tune to any open chord
2. How to play steel guitar in any key, with an open tonic chord

HARMONICS

G Tuning

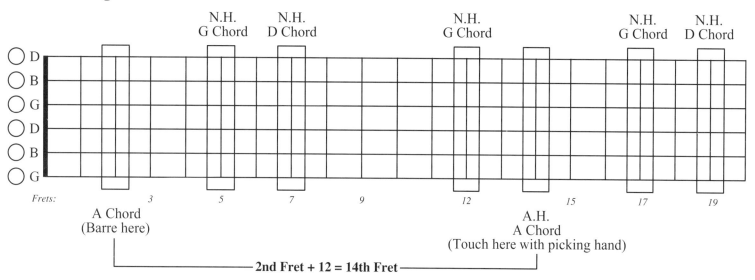

| | N.H. G Chord | N.H. D Chord | | N.H. G Chord | | N.H. G Chord | N.H. D Chord |

Frets: 3 5 7 9 12 15 17 19

A Chord (Barre here)

A.H. A Chord (Touch here with picking hand)

— 2nd Fret + 12 = 14th Fret —

WHY? Harmonics add color and variety to solos and backup. Steel players have been using them since the earliest recordings of lap guitars.

WHAT? **Harmonics are the bell-like notes that you get by lightly touching the strings at certain strategic places before picking them. ROADMAP #12** shows where to touch the strings for harmonics.

Natural harmonics are played by touching or barring strings with your fretting hand at the places marked "N.H." in **ROADMAP #12**. There are other places to play natural harmonics, but these are the easiest spots.

Artificial harmonics are played by touching or barring strings with the picking hand, as in the sample A chord that is marked "A.H." in **ROADMAP #12**.

Natural harmonics can be played only at certain places on the fretboard, but any note can be played with artificial harmonics.

HOW? **To play natural harmonics, touch the strings lightly with the side of the pinky of your fretting hand, as shown in this photo:**

- Once they are "fretted" at the right place, pick the strings as usual.
- Instantly remove your fretting hand from the strings after picking them, or the sound will be muted.
- To get a clear, bell-like chime, touch the strings right over the 12th-fret markings.
- If you do all of this correctly, it will sound like the following example:

G Tuning

TRACK 57

- Notice that the two D chords in **ROADMAP #12** sound the same, but the G chord at the fifth fret is an octave higher than the G chord at the 12th fret.
- **In D tuning, as in G tuning, the fifth and 12th frets give you natural harmonics for the I chord; the seventh and 19th frets give you natural harmonics for the V chord.** (In the key of D, the I chord is D and the V chord is A.)

To play artificial harmonics:

- Fret two or three strings as usual, with the steel.
- Touch the strings 12 frets above the fret point with the side of your picking hand, as shown in Photo 1 below.
- Pick the strings with the thumb of your picking hand.
- Immediately remove the side of your hand from the strings after picking them so that they will not be muted.
- Play an artificial harmonic on a single string by "fretting" it with the ring finger of your picking hand and picking it with your thumb (which is curled under the ring finger), as shown in Photo 2 below.

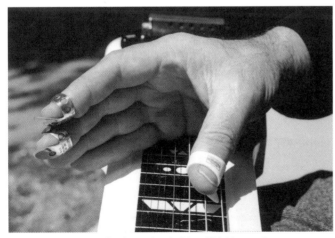

Photo 1: Playing a chord with artificial harmonics

Photo 2: Playing a single string with artificial harmonic

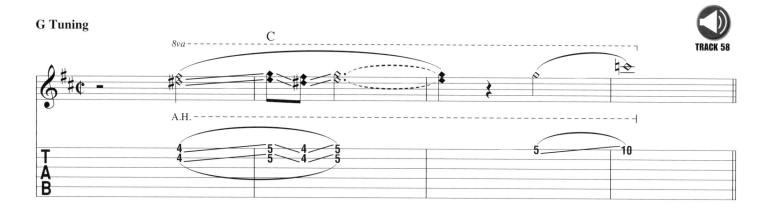
DO IT!   Play "Chimes," below, an instrumental that features artificial and natural harmonics:

CHIMES

TRACK 59

SUMMING UP—NOW YOU KNOW...

1. How to play certain chords or single notes with natural harmonics

2. How to play any chord or single note with artificial harmonics

USING THE PRACTICE TRACKS

On the four practice tracks, the lap steel is separated from the rest of the band—it's on just one side of your stereo. You can tune it out and use the band as backup, trying out any soloing techniques that you like, in any tuning. You can also imitate the steel solos. Here are the soloing ideas on each track:

PRACTICE TRACK #60: 12-BAR BLUES/ROCK IN G AND D (G TUNING)

TRACK 60

This one goes four times around a 12-bar blues.

- During the first 12 bars, the solo consists of first-position G blues licks.

- In the second 12 bars, the solo consists of moveable G blues licks at the 12th fret.

- In the third 12 bars, the solo follows the chord changes, with licks based on each barred chord.

- The fourth time, the tune modulates to the key of D and the solo is built around moveable blues scales. The solo follows the tune's chord changes, with licks based on the various barred chords.

PRACTICE TRACK #61: "THE WATER IS WIDE" IN D (G TUNING)

TRACK 61

Playing twice around this 16-bar tune, the soloist offers many examples of how to play minor chords. Here's the progression:

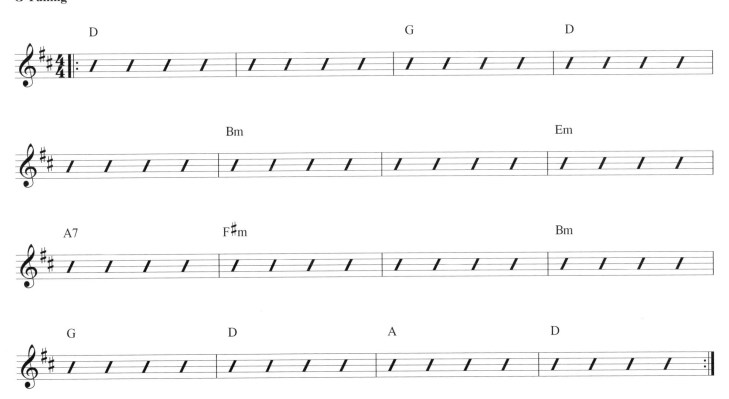

PRACTICE TRACK #62: 8-BAR BLUES SHUFFLE IN D AND E (D AND E7 TUNINGS)

TRACK 62

The track goes around this 8-bar blues three times in D tuning, in the key of D, and twice in E7 tuning, in the key of E. Here's what the soloist is doing:

- Eight bars of first-position D blues licks

- Eight bars of moveable D blues licks at the 12th fret

- Eight bars of moveable licks based on barred chords, using a barred chord for each chord change

- 16 bars of improvisation in E7 tuning, in the key of E

Here's the basic progression in both keys (D and E):

D Tuning

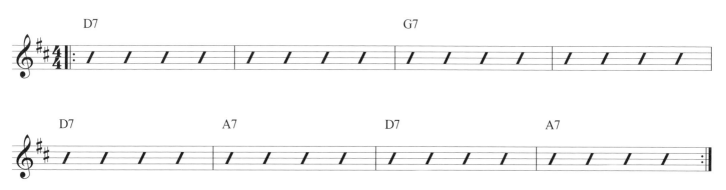

E7 Tuning

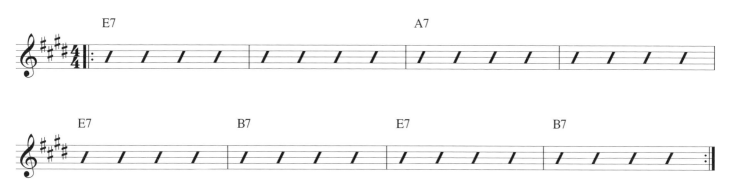

PRACTICE TRACK #63: WESTERN SWING TUNE IN C

This 32-bar tune is played three times, first in E7 tuning, then twice in C6 tuning. The soloist plays chord-based licks:

C7 Tuning and C6 Tuning

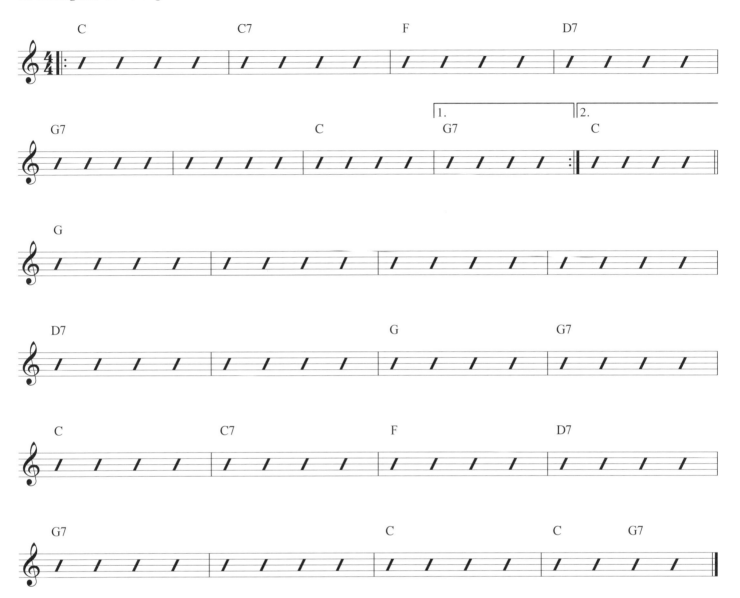

LISTENING SUGGESTIONS

Whatever musical genre interests you, it's always a good idea to become familiar with the pioneers and innovators who developed and popularized the styles and techniques associated with that genre. Here's an incomplete but essential list of important electric lap-steel players who helped shape the development of the instrument:

Bob Dunn joined the pioneer Western swing band Milton Brown and His Musical Brownies in the early '30s. Famous for his jazzy, horn-like phrasing, he's also credited with designing one of the first electric instruments when he amplified his acoustic guitar. He's one of the first players to make electric lap guitar a viable instrument.

Sol Ho'opi'i, a Hawaiian who took up electric lap steel in the mid '30s, was also one of the first electric lap-steelers. His jazzy style was heard by millions, not only in thousands of pop, country, and swing recordings, but in the many Hollywood movies in which he played. He developed the C#m tuning, also called "E13" (it's just like E7, with the second string raised to C#).

Noel Boggs, a premiere Western swing steeler, played with Hank Penny, Bob Wills, Spade Cooley, and many others in '30s and '40s (including the Sons of the Pioneers, Roy Rogers, and Gene Autry). A friend of Charlie Christian, he memorized many of Christian's solos and employed the guitarist's modern, jazzy phrasing when he arranged some of Western swing's first harmonized, three-instrument solos. These harmonized, bebop-styled "heads" of songs became a staple of the genre. Also a friend of Leo Fender, Boggs played the first Fender steel guitar.

Leon McAuliffe is known to Western swing fans because of Bob Wills's frequent "Take it away, Leon!" interjections on recordings. He played with Wills in one of the first Western swing bands, the Light Crust Doughboys, in the early '30s and was a key member of Wills' own band, the Texas Playboys. His "Steel Guitar Rag" is an essential lap-steel instrumental, and he was one of the first to use multi-neck guitars.

Jerry Byrd is one of the most influential lap-steelers. He was very important to the development of the instrument, especially in country music. A chief architect of the Nashville Sound, he worked with Chet Atkins, Marty Robbins, Hank Snow, Ernest Tubb, Red Foley, Hank Williams, and many others throughout the '40s and '50s. He developed C6 tuning and, in thousands of recordings, both as a sideman and a featured artist, his style and licks helped define what lap steel could do in country music.

Joaquin Murphey played and recorded with Western swing players like Spade Cooley, Tex Williams, T. Texas Tyler, and others throughout the '40s and '50s, popularizing his very jazzy approach to lap steel.

Don Helms played with Hank Williams throughout the '40s and with many country stars after Williams's death (Patsy Cline, Lefty Frizzell, Johnny Cash, etc.). Williams's recordings may be the most influential in country music history, so Helms's playing has had a major influence, as well. He's famous for playing in the upper octaves, as producer Fred Rose kept telling him to "play higher up the neck!"

Alvino Rey, a pioneering swing guitarist and lap-steeler in the '30s and '40s, created a guitar amplifier in the '20s, but failed to patent it! He also helped Gibson develop the pickup for their first electric guitar and is credited with inventing the pedal steel when he added pedals to his lap instrument. Rey led his own swing band in the '40s, playing steel and exposing a nationwide urban audience to the instrument via radio and television shows, touring, hit records, and movie appearances.

David Lindley backed Jackson Browne throughout the '70s. Since then, he has played and recorded with countless pop, rock, and R&B stars, spreading the gospel of lap steel and its use in many genres. With his bluegrass and old-time music background and experience playing with so many artists of different musical stripes, he has also become a practitioner of "world music" in his eclectic solo performances and recordings. Lindley has often collaborated with **Ry Cooder**, whose lap-steel playing on movie soundtracks like *Paris, Texas* has helped popularize the instrument.

Freddie Roulette and **Sonny Rhodes** are two blues lap-steel stars who prove how effective the instrument can be in that genre.

Some mention must be made of "sacred steel," an amazing African-American gospel music style that has kept lap steels singing since the '30s. To get your feet wet in sacred steel, listen to **Aubrey Ghent** and **Sonny Treadway**.

ABOUT THE AUTHOR

Fred Sokolow is best-known as the author of over 150 instructional and transcription books and DVDs for guitar, banjo, Dobro, mandolin, lap steel, and ukulele. Fred has long been a well-known West Coast multi-string performer and recording artist, particularly on the acoustic music scene. The diverse musical genres covered in his books and DVDs, along with several bluegrass, jazz, and rock CDs that he has released, demonstrate his mastery of many musical styles. Whether he's playing Delta bottleneck blues, bluegrass, old-time banjo, '30s swing guitar, or screaming rock solos, he does it with authenticity and passion.

Other books from Fred that may be of interest:

- *Fretboard Roadmaps for Dobro*
  (book/audio), Hal Leonard

- *Fretboard Roadmaps for Slide Guitar*
  (book/audio), Hal Leonard

- *Fretboard Roadmaps for Guitar*, Second
  Edition (book/audio), Hal Leonard

You can contact Fred with questions about this book, or any of his other instruction books or DVDs, by visiting his website, *sokolowmusic.com*.

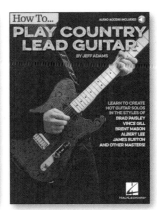
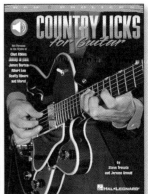

Guitar Instruction
Country Style!
from Hal Leonard

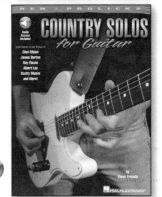

CHICKEN PICKIN' • *by Eric Halbig*

INCLUDES TAB

This book provides a "bird's-eye-view" of the techniques and licks common to playing hot, country lead guitar! Covers over 100 hot country guitar licks: open-string licks, double-stop licks, scales, string bending, repetitive sequences, and chromatic licks. The online audio includes 99 demonstration tracks with each lick performed at two tempos.

00695599 Book/Online Audio $17.99

DANIEL DONATO – THE NEW MASTER OF THE TELECASTER

INCLUDES TAB **DVD**

PATHWAYS TO DYNAMIC SOLOS

This exclusive instructional book and DVD set includes guitar lessons taught by young Nashville phenom Daniel Donato. The "New Master of the Telecaster" shows you his unique "pathways" concept, opening your mind and fingers to uninhibited fretboard freedom, increased music theory comprehension, and more dynamic solos! The DVD features Daniel Donato himself providing full-band performances and a full hour of guitar lessons, The book includes guitar tab for all the DVD lessons and performances. Topics covered include: using chromatic notes • application of bends • double stops • analyzing different styles • and more. DVD running time: 1 hr., 4 min.

00121923 Book/DVD Pack $19.99

FRETBOARD ROADMAPS – COUNTRY GUITAR

INCLUDES TAB

The Essential Patterns That All the Pros Know and Use • by Fred Sokolow

This book/CD pack will teach you how to play lead and rhythm in the country style anywhere on the fretboard in any key. You'll play basic country progressions, boogie licks, steel licks, and other melodies and licks. You'll also learn a variety of lead guitar styles using moveable scale patterns, sliding scale patterns, chord-based licks, double-note licks, and more. The book features easy-to-follow diagrams and instructions for beginning, intermediate, and advanced players.

00695353 Book/CD Pack $16.99

HOW TO PLAY COUNTRY LEAD GUITAR

INCLUDES TAB

by Jeff Adams

Here is a comprehensive stylistic breakdown of country guitar techniques from the past 50 years. Drawing inspiration from the timelessly innovative licks of Merle Travis, Chet Atkins, Albert Lee, Vince Gill, Brent Mason and Brad Paisley, the near 90 musical examples within these pages will hone your left and right hands with technical string-bending and rolling licks while sharpening your knowledge of the thought process behind creating your own licks, and why and when to play them.

00131103 Book/Online Audio $19.99

COUNTRY LICKS FOR GUITAR

INCLUDES TAB

by Steve Trovato and Jerome Arnold

This unique package examines the lead guitar licks of the masters of country guitar, such as Chet Atkins, Jimmy Bryant, James Burton, Albert Lee, Scotty Moore, and many others! The online audio includes demonstrations of each lick at normal and slow speeds. The instruction covers single-string licks, pedal-steel licks, open-string licks, chord licks, rockabilly licks, funky country licks, tips on fingerings, phrasing, technique, theory, and application.

00695577 Book/Online Audo $19.99

COUNTRY SOLOS FOR GUITAR

INCLUDES TAB

by Steve Trovato

This unique book/audio pack lets guitarists examine the solo styles of axe masters such as Chet Atkins, James Burton, Ray Flacke, Albert Lee, Scotty Moore, Roy Nichols, Jerry Reed and others. It covers techniques including hot banjo rolls, funky double stops, pedal-steel licks, open-string licks and more, in standard notation and tab with phrase-by-phrase performance notes. The online audio includes full demonstrations and rhythm-only tracks.

00695448 Book/Online Audio $19.99

RED-HOT COUNTRY GUITAR

by Michael Hawley

The complete guide to playing lead guitar in the styles of Pete Anderson, Danny Gatton, Albert Lee, Brent Mason, and more. Includes loads of red-hot licks, techniques, solos, theory and more.

00695831 Book/Online Audio $19.99

25 GREAT COUNTRY GUITAR SOLOS

INCLUDES TAB

by Dave Rubin

Provides solo transcriptions in notes & tab, lessons on how to play them, guitarist bios, equipment notes, photos, history, and much more. The CD contains full-band demos of every solo in the book. Songs include: Country Boy • Foggy Mountain Special • Folsom Prison Blues • Hellecaster Theme • Hello Mary Lou • I've Got a Tiger by the Tail • The Only Daddy That Will Walk the Line • Please, Please Baby • Sugarfoot Rag • and more.

00699926 Book/CD Pack $19.99

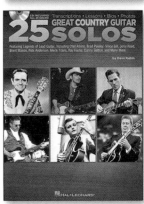

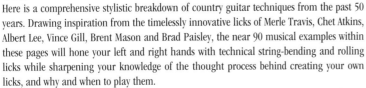